From The Inside

From The Inside
A Backdrop to the Music of My Life

Russ DiBella

AuthorHouse™
1663 Liberty Drive
Bloomington, IN 47403
www.authorhouse.com
Phone: 1-800-839-8640

© *2011 Russ DiBella. All rights reserved.*

No part of this book may be reproduced, stored in a retrieval system, or transmitted by any means without the written permission of the author.

First published by AuthorHouse 02/28/2011

ISBN: 978-1-4567-1519-9 (sc)
ISBN: 978-1-4567-1517-5 (hc)
ISBN: 978-1-4567-1518-2 (e)

Library of Congress Control Number: 2011903225

Printed in the United States of America

Cover and interior photos taken by the author except for page 203 which was originally taken by Dan Hopper (www.danhoppermedia.com)

Any people depicted in stock imagery provided by Thinkstock are models, and such images are being used for illustrative purposes only.

This book is printed on acid-free paper.

Because of the dynamic nature of the Internet, any Web addresses or links contained in this book may have changed since publication and may no longer be valid. The views expressed in this work are solely those of the author and do not necessarily reflect the views of the publisher, and the publisher hereby disclaims any responsibility for them.

To Kelley, Alea and Kelsey for the patience

To Dad and Mom for the music

To my bandmates for the journey

*All my life I've looked at words
as though I were seeing them for the first time
— Ernest Hemingway*

*Without music, life would be a mistake
— Friedrich Nietzsche*

Introduction ix

A PASSION REVEALED

1: Discovery 1
2: A World of Drums 9
3: It All Began With Boston 15
4: Front & Center with Cheap Trick 21
5: Genesis: A New Perspective 27
6: A Quiet Riot in California 33
7: The Mission… and Other Assorted Stuff 37
8: REO Speedwagon / Survivor: Making Connections 41
9: Musical Chairs 47
10: Live Aid: History in the Making 57
11: 2nd Annual MTV Video Music Awards 71
12: Bon Jovi: Incoming! 79
13: Local Shots: 1980s Philly 81
14: John Mellencamp: Backstage Moments 97
15: A Van Halen Soundcheck 101

BELONGING THERE

16: A Return to Rush 109
17: Journey / Def Leppard 121
18: The David Lee Roth Radio Show 127
19: Rush: The Trilogy 133
20: Coming 'Round Again 143
21: Taking It to the Next Level 149
22: Dave Matthews Band 153
23: Tim McGraw / Jason Aldean: Country Gentlemen 157
24: Maidens, Pearls and Chicago Doobies 161
25: A Mötley Festival of Singers, Songwriters, Priests and Eagles 171
26: Toby Keith / Montgomery Gentry 185
27: Kid Rock / Lynyrd Skynyrd: Southern-Fried Rock 189
28: Journey / Heart / Cheap Trick: Stage Right 193
29: Putting Down the Sticks 203

EVERYTHING AFTER

30:	Bruce Springsteen: The Spectrum Revisited	207
31:	No Doubt	213
32:	Jimmy Buffett: Margarainyville	215
33:	A Pause for Perspective	219
34:	Def Leppard / Poison / Cheap Trick: Stage Right II	223
35:	August and (almost) Everything After	231
36:	A KISS Soundcheck	243
37:	AC/DC: The Final Act	249
38:	Rush: Une Autre! Un Rappel! Encore!	253
	Conclusion	259
	Acknowledgements	263
	Final Fun Facts	267
	References	271

Introduction

When words leave off, music begins
— Heinrich Heine

For as long as I can remember I've had creative leanings; an innate and seemingly boundless drive to make something from nothing. Whether practical or artistic, physical or conceptual; the process was always as enjoyable as the result. And when I discovered a heightened sense of gratification from one interest more than all others, I became somewhat of an enthusiast.

It was an early attraction to words that found me exploring the worlds of poetry, prose and lyrics to varying degrees throughout my life; metaphorically taking me on some very rewarding personal, educational and artistic journeys. And though my penchant for creating has proven both varied and long-lasting, it's been my relationship with words that has remained the constant.

In a simultaneous extension of my lyrical pursuits an active discovery of music — of drumming in particular — broadened my horizons and provided a new and equally gratifying outlet for me. Performance became the physical manifestation of my writing when I assumed the role of lyricist in Upper Level — a band formed with some long-time friends and fellow musicians. This was one of the most enjoyable musical periods for me as writing, drumming and singing as well as collaborating on the music and arrangements satisfied my creative needs in every way. Writing and playing would become almost indistinguishable; complementing and feeding off one another as that particular aspect of my life began to take shape.

As music continued to be my diversion of choice (though it seems as if *it* had actually chosen *me*), I soon merged that with a secondary focus on preserving all music-related items and ephemera. An assortment of music magazines, concert tickets and occasional tour programs would serve not only as the inception of a slightly more developed adaptation of this sideline interest but also as a personal perspective on my experiences from the past three decades; each ticket in particular a small record of when and where I was at different intervals on the long and winding musical road.

In time throughout varying stages of interest I had amassed a relatively unassuming but personally significant collection of memorabilia — with a focus on drumsticks — from numerous concerts and pre-shows. And when I decided to chronicle these events and all peripherally-related activities, it was in part this collection that would offer inspiration for and provide verification of much that had occurred.

For the next few years I became immersed in this very specific place from my past and present; testing the accuracy of memory, the limits of fatigue and my ability to piece together what essentially amounts to my story... so far.

Part I:
A PASSION REVEALED

*Turn the pages
See the faces that we've known
All the memories held within are not our own
Shared among the ones who've long since come and gone
Time rolls on…*

A MATTER OF TIME / 2005

ONE
Discovery

Age is a matter of feeling, not of years
— *George William Curtis*

Forty came surprisingly early to me, at least insofar as how good I felt both physically and mentally. Not that I necessarily knew what it should feel like nor did I believe I was any less mature than a man my age should be — my penchant for Sunday comics and animated sitcoms notwithstanding. I've always been dedicated to my responsibilities as husband, father and professional and maintain an otherwise plausibly adult attitude toward life in general. But with respect to music, my interest in the ancillary aspects of the artists has remained as fervent as when I first dropped a needle on an album back in middle school.

Early on in those teenage years a fair amount of discretionary time was available to indulge and easily become immersed in newly revealed interests. What was once uninhibited childhood curiosity about all things new (because all things *were* new) soon became teenage inquisitiveness; more mature and somewhat more focused. Moments of self-defining exploration and discovery began to take shape and, in some cases, take hold. And when one of those interests gripped me compellingly I became engaged to the extent that even a cursory glance would have elicited a reasonable assumption of endurance; perhaps even of lifelong measure.

And just as I found *my* passion so, too, did a number of friends realize their own. Although some have maintained to varying degrees the intensity felt in those early days, a few even having uncovered new and lasting diversions along the way, many others seem to have all too easily relinquished their initial enthusiasm as though mere infatuation. Regardless of category, interests that once seemed as concentrated as mine were casually dismissed by most as they made their way into adulthood.

But that was obviously not the case with me; my interest in learning about music actually having increased and broadened over the years as my curiosity about the details continued and eventually led to other more interactive pursuits. Age may have crept up on me but it was clearly not a factor in my love of all things music. And with regard to all that would follow it would appear as though I had yet to graduate from those hallowed halls of youth. Yet here I am chronologically — and seemingly suddenly — more than three times older.

As Sherwin B. Nuland states in *The Art of Aging: A Doctor's Prescription for Well-Being:* "So gradual a progression is the onset of our aging that we one day find it to be fully upon us."

As a supplement to this realization it's my belief that growing *older* does not necessarily mean growing *up.* Though we ultimately have no choice about the former (if we're fortunate), we can still be respected and contributing members of society while suspending the latter — within reason, of course.

I recall a moment from my mid-twenties as I was scanning the pages of *Rolling Stone* magazine at a local convenience store. A former high school acquaintance I hadn't seen since graduation walked in and quickly recognized me. Seeing the magazine in my hands and knowing my musical background he shook his head scornfully while asking in a derisory tone, "You still *read* those things?" Though I knew his question was essentially rhetorical, the pause in his step seemed to indicate an anticipated reply. But I felt no obligation to dignify his words with response, taking far more pleasure in my silent rebuff.

From The Inside

Sir Francis Bacon once said: "In taking revenge, a man is but even with his enemy; but in passing it over, he is superior."

Looking down again I continued reading and he simply walked away.

His apparent disdain, however, had me wondering why such an in-depth interest in this particular genre of entertainment is looked upon as juvenile or inappropriate later in life while similar attention paid to other areas of entertainment; professional sports in particular, is widely accepted (I don't recall ever painting my face to cheer on a favorite band or going bare-chested in winter to a concert). In fact, it's almost shocking *not* to be interested in sports; especially as an adult male, and I wondered if he would have asked that question had I been reading *Sports Illustrated* instead of *Rolling Stone*. Though none of this is meant to offend sports fans (many of whom I call family and friends), the double standard makes no sense to me. Likewise, it's of no concern.

Ever since those middle school days for the most part neither time nor responsibility diminished my interest to any discernible degree. From that point forward although the music remained most important, it was never enough simply to listen to records; I had to read every lyric, liner note and credit as well as scrutinize any other information printed on the album jackets or inner sleeves — sometimes even before purchasing them when friends and I would hang out at a small local record shop (typically second among musicians only to stores selling musical instruments) called The Comfort Station; a name I initially thought was by design both skillfully vague and subtly appropriate for a music store. But, as I was quick to discover, it was actually named for the owner — Barbara Comfort (so much for my insightfulness).

Fun Fact: Although I long wondered why a caricature of an outhouse was used alongside the name of the store, I would years later learn that the term "comfort station" is actually a reference to such a facility — one of which is so notable (as part of the Department of Conservation and Recreation's Trailside Museum in Milton, MA) that it's actually listed on the National Register of Historic Places.

~~~~

Although I stopped short of joining any fan clubs, wanting to know as much as possible about the bands, their music and the recordings became an almost essential part of the overall experience. Taking special note of the crossover among certain producers, engineers, songwriters, session musicians and even studios used by various bands or artists I'd admired provided further insight and intrigued me beyond the music. And as an optimistically budding drummer at the time I was even further inspired to dig deeper; to see what may lie ahead in a potential life of music for *me*.

In those very pre-Internet days additional information about favorite bands could often only be gleaned from magazines such as *Rolling Stone*, *Hit Parader*, *Creem* and later *Spin* (save the occasional biography). Friends and I would often idle away our time at the local 7-Eleven convenience store poring over these magazines as if on loan from the town library. On occasion when one or two had enough good pictures and stories or, better yet, when they included interviews with any of my favorite bands, they'd be deemed worthy of purchase. But in an ironic twist it would be that very distinction which resulted in their eventual — and deliberate — demolition as various pictures were culled from the pages to grace the walls of my bedroom while others became a veritable palette from which I'd create a variety of collages and school art projects. These, too, would eventually end up on my walls. It seemed no matter the task at hand, whenever possible, music would be the inspired focal point.

As a good student, albeit somewhat detached from an intrinsic desire to learn the more mundane subject matter, employing the creative process and working within the familiar and respected framework of music helped make the assignments much more enjoyable for me. As my interest in writing developed I casually branched out into poetry and even more intensely into lyrics; both styles lending themselves well to my songwriting efforts during the next few decades.

So here I am in my mid-forties, still listening to and playing music as much as possible and expanding my writing yet again — this time in the form of a memoir of sorts. Although I've written other less time-consuming, less in-depth pieces either as college coursework, personal projects or professional assignments, this was the first undertaking of its kind (and magnitude) for me and once again I found myself playing to my strengths and working within a structure that served me so well in the past. But this time, strangely enough, music as the subject was not entirely my idea.

Coincidentally, at a time when I was eager to begin a new writing project and quietly considering topics, some friends suggested individually that I document all the more noteworthy musical moments of my life. Knowing well many of those moments and even having shared in a few, they thought the idea a good one and I agreed, immediately setting out on a journey which has given me retrospection on more than thirty years.

Perhaps the most interesting aspect about the process was discovering that until I found the perfect words to express the memories, I hadn't fully appreciated them for what they were — a backdrop to my life of music. And despite my rather lucid recollections of the experiences, having verbally recounted them many times throughout the years, it was the act of putting them down on paper that assisted in their refinement. As a purist accuracy was important to me and, as such, in the absence of information I didn't want imagination filling the gaps. So I cross-checked details against facts from several sources; old concert tickets, tour programs, albums, websites and even discussions with anyone who shared in the experiences. Those meticulous processes served me well and helped capture or confirm many of the finer points story by story; a method I imagine would work well for most detail-oriented writing projects.

Consider a childhood account related by Anne Lamott in her book *Bird by Bird: Some Instructions on Writing and Life:* "Thirty years ago my older brother was trying to get a report on birds written. It was due the next day and he was immobilized by the hugeness of the task ahead. Then my father sat down beside him, put his arm around my brother's shoulder and said, 'Bird by bird, buddy. Just take it bird by bird.'"

An added benefit to this attention-to-detail approach was that it triggered memories that had otherwise slipped through the proverbial cracks in my mind — at one point calling them up at such a rate that, oddly enough, I felt the more I wrote the further I was from finishing.

But as any writer knows; a wealth of information and too many ideas are the exception to the rule — or at the very least a welcome predicament. So I felt good about the position I was in with regard to how much material my experiences would provide. Nevertheless, I wasn't quite as confident about how I'd arrange them into some form of flowing narrative; translation onto paper with a secondary goal of appealing to a broad audience. Though that second part is never undemanding (nor is there any formula for its realization), the words soon came together as I moved further into the outline stage and a larger form began to materialize, almost of its own accord. All I had to do then was begin.

It's been said about writing that simply beginning is to be half done as there are often extensive periods spent waiting for inspiration to strike. But as ironically illustrated in my 1989 ballad-style poem *The Blank Page*, sometimes even the lack of a topic can prove to be valid subject matter.

With my theme having been defined, a big picture taking shape and the beginning of my account unfolding agreeably, I guess it could be said that I'm half done. Well... maybe not quite *half.*

The Blank Page

I stare at the page in front of me
So blank — or so it seems
No words are calling out to me
No loud whispers or quiet screams

No poetry with rhyme or reason
No humor or interesting plot
This just doesn't seem to be working
Nothing's coming and something is not

Yet soon I know I'll have something
And whether it's good or it's bad
At that point at least I'll know one thing
That it's certainly more than I had

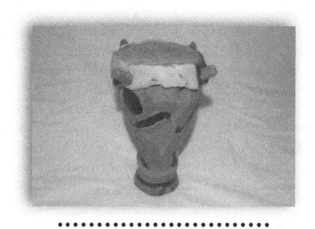

TWO
A World of Drums

If thine enemy wrong thee, buy each of his children a drum
— Chinese Proverb

Growing up in a large and somewhat musical family, the fourth of five children, I was passively introduced to music by way of my parents; their individual abilities pleasantly ever present throughout my childhood and adolescence. It was this familiarity that led me to believe music in the home was likely the norm. Only after experiencing the home lives of friends, however, did I discover it was actually the exception to the rule; the occasional idle or seldom-visited piano sadly more often a piece of ornamental furniture than a musical instrument.

But exposure to music also came in other ways when my three older sisters dabbled in it at various times long before I took an interest (although admittedly I wanted to be David Cassidy from The Partridge Family when I was quite young — but that's another story). I recall to varying degrees their individual efforts; my oldest sister Diane's very impressive song and dance routine to *Cabaret* for a county-wide pageant on her high school stage (the same stage on which I would perform with my band Thrust years later), Carole's flirtation with classical guitar (the first one I ever attempted to play) and Kathleen's brief dalliance with the clarinet and her far more lasting and beloved pursuit of singing — in the church choir, the school choral group and at wedding ceremonies (including her own when she sang Lulu's *To Sir, With Love* to our father at her reception). Although the youngest of the brood, Michael, would escape without any apparent active interest in music it's doubtful these memories are any less vivid to him as music permeated our household. It was an infusion that would eventually seep into my life, root firmly and flourish.

My father, Russ, a leisure-pursuit yet accomplished pianist and accordionist, was selected to appear on the *All-Navy Toast of the Town Ed Sullivan Show* in 1955. My mother, Sally, a gifted vocalist, has been a leading member of the church choir for as long as I can remember. Our home was often filled with the sounds of their respective talents; dad's melodic renditions of the classics emanating from his old Kohler & Campbell console piano and mom's favorite church hymns and other familiar songs of the day sung acapella whenever the mood would strike her.

Almost always on, the radio was a complement to these impromptu live performances and would introduce me at the time to the music of Elvis Presley, Dionne Warwick and Frank Sinatra among many others. Although I'd later discover in more detail the connection between music and memory, unbeknownst to me it was already placing date stamps on my mind. I would be twelve years old when Presley would die, seventeen when I took my first plane trip — to San Jose, CA — reminding me of Warwick's 1968 hit — the Burt Bacharach / Hal David-penned *Do You Know the Way to San Jose*, and thirty-three when Sinatra would pass away. Although all of this music was a relative constant, neither of my parents pointed me in a musical direction. But following a seemingly negligible twist of fate I discovered a tendency for it and in my pursuit found both of them to be quite supportive. It was then that I began a musical journey that under previous conditions may have simply gone unexplored.

Fun Fact: Inspired by the purpose of this book and having never seen my father's accordion performance of the 1931 song *Lady of Spain* on the Ed Sullivan Show (nobody in my family had seen it, except perhaps my father's parents and sisters back when it first aired), I set out to locate a copy. My quest began on the Internet searching YouTube for any Ed Sullivan clips and it fell into place rather quickly after discovering a Pickens Sisters performance from the early 50s. I contacted the person who posted that clip (the granddaughter of one of the Sisters as it turns out) and she provided me with the name of the company who owns the rights to all the Ed Sullivan shows. I got in touch with them, advised them of approximately when my father was on and waited. Within a week I received word they had found the clip and that it was in great audio and video condition. I immediately bought a copy and had it in my hands by the following week. What would have otherwise been a lost piece of very interesting family history — to me at least — was unearthed after fifty-three years and shared with my father as a surprise for his seventy-fifth birthday (much to his grateful astonishment), with my mother (who was in the audience during his performance as they had just begun dating) and with my wife, daughters, siblings, aunts and uncles.

~~~~~

In our childhood and teenage years in the small, historically-rich town of Medford, NJ my friends and I would play stick ball or street hockey, hang out at the local swimming pool, go canoeing in the lakes or casually ride bikes to nowhere in particular in an effort to pass the seemingly endless days of summer. Throughout the falls and winters we'd engage in organized sports and shoulder the typical responsibilities of school work and chores all while navigating our way through adolescence trying to create some semblance of an as yet undefined social life. Through it all most of us would simply go along only occasionally and halfheartedly testing the universal waters of teenage rebellion. It was the standard stuff of youth in Medford just as in most small towns anywhere else in America and only time, effort or unforeseen circumstances would put a wrinkle in the fabric of that routine.

During the summer of 1977 a minor disruption in my adolescent life became a major turning point for me that involved a shift from a sideline interest in sports to one of music. A slight falling out with a friend had me widening my outlook and I began to spend more time with some guys I knew from school. Dan Hopper was one of those guys and not long after meeting we discovered a similar interest in music; one that would grow commensurately with our friendship during the next several years of middle school, high school and beyond.

One of the first manifestations of this common bond took place during Halloween that year when Dan, mutual friends Paul Paetow and Mike DiDio and I decided to dress up for the night's festivities. The costumes of choice were those of the hard rock band KISS.

Formed in New York City in the early 70s, the band was known as much for their face paint and flamboyance as for their theatrical and pyrotechnic-filled live shows. Though somewhat new to their music at the time, I would soon become even more familiar with it, eventually seeing them in concert at the Spectrum on September 7, 1979. With Dan as guitarist Ace Frehley and two of the three remaining members having already been accounted for by Paul and Mike prior to me joining their circle; I took the final slot as drummer Peter Criss. It was this chance role that I somewhat credit as one of the reasons I eventually began playing the drums; this slight initial exposure perhaps having fanned an ember of intuitive awareness in some emergent musical recess of my mind.

While scanning the pages of *Modern Drummer* magazine in early 1978, I came across a Ludwig Drum advertisement offering a free pair of drumsticks. Though not yet a drummer, reading the magazine was an early step in my then-hopeful pursuit as learning about drummers I'd admired and even some I'd never heard of further encouraged my newfound interest. I soon discovered that the reciprocal was equally true; the more knowledgeable I became about drumming overall, the more I wanted to learn about those in the field. After cutting out the ad and filling in the requisite name and address information I sent it off in eager anticipation of what was to come. Sure it was only a pair of sticks; two cylindrically-shaped pieces of wood of nominal value. But just thirteen years old at the time to me they were a thing of beauty; a tangible bridge of sorts to an exciting new world of music… a world of *drums!*

Fun Fact: Long before I took an interest in music my father gave me a small novelty drum he bought while on a business trip. I've maintained to this day the initial fondness I felt for it, careful never to lose it in all the years since. Its unique shape, hand-painted designs, animal skin membrane (held firmly in place by protruding pegs) and sound were fascinatingly weird and wonderful to my young eyes and ears. Curious about those characteristics in more recent years, I did some research and discovered it to be a crude replica of an African Zigua drum. Played by hand, they were used in Tanzania during sacred healing rituals; perhaps in an early form of drum therapy (an ancient approach that uses rhythm to promote healing). Though I'm not sure why my father chose a drum of all things, it would years later prove interestingly prophetic. As the oldest piece of music-related memorabilia I own, it's now proudly and aptly displayed in my music room.

In seemingly no time at all the sticks arrived and, as anticipated, I fell upon them with enthusiasm. After examining them, taking note of the imprinted Ludwig logo and becoming aware of how "right" they felt in my hands, I soon put them to good use beating on a pillow in cadence with the albums playing on my turntable. I still wasn't a drummer and my bedroom was hardly Carnegie Hall, but this initial and unrefined experience gave me a sense that I was at least one step closer to both.

The excitement I felt getting that first pair of sticks is why it remains one of my more inimitable musical memories. That I soon began taking lessons, playing actual drums (a Blue Sparkle, no-name, five-piece kit found in the local classified ads) and that music grew to be an important part of my life certainly added a new level of appreciation for that moment. What those sticks ostensibly came to represent and how they eventually led to all the bands I played in, innumerable concerts I attended and memories created via my ad hoc hobby of drumstick collecting (coupled with occasional opportunities of artist interaction) helped define a life of music as both enthusiast and accomplice.

More than thirty years later music is still an integral part of who I am; perhaps the most identifiable attribute with respect to those who know me best. I'm still drumming, playing guitar, writing and recording songs and actively attending concerts with an ever-watchful eye (give or take the occasional lapse) on how to catch a glimpse into the inner workings of a live concert setting and — as always — how to get that next drumstick.

At this point it's probably best to include a bit of perspective on the following sequence of events as their continuation in my life may appear to be merely a result of latent adolescence — although admittedly I've never denied carrying a fair amount of *that* into adulthood. But in reality these experiences are more an extension of my passion for music and the artists I've come to appreciate. I've always had a healthy appetite for looking beneath the surface to see how things work; to get a better understanding of them from the inside out. I've also long maintained an inherent desire to connect more deeply with people and things that resonate with me. So when music became part of my life and I began attending concerts more frequently, those two characteristics naturally applied and I began to explore the world of live music from a different perspective; a backstage view as it were. It was a seemingly innate drive to experience more than the usual; to pass through the literal and figurative turnstiles through which relatively few get to pass.

As a disclaimer of sorts, even though I used mild deception on occasion to carry out many of these activities it was always harmless, never disruptive and all in good fun. But regardless, this *was* rock'n'roll and a fair amount of lunacy should be accepted — if not expected.

THREE
It All Began With Boston

October 30, 1978

Music is the art which is most nigh to tears and memory
— Oscar Wilde

In a logical extension of my new interest in drumming a teenage rite of passage soon took place — attending my first concert. As with many other musical firsts in my life I remember this show as one of those defining moments that settled comfortably and appropriately in my long-term memory along with The Doobie Brothers' *What a Fool Believes*, Bob Lapata and a show at Mike DiDio's house (my first 45-rpm record, drum teacher and band gig respectively). Though only thirteen years old at the time and when discovery was taking many forms, I recall feeling that this was one of the more noteworthy ones. Not because it was yet another musical experience, but because of my awareness that a passion had been revealed. From my early and varied exposure to music to an eventual foray into drumming, this live show was another first that confirmed that passion. Of course there were many other firsts to come; some music related, some not. As for the latter, I'm frequently able to correlate them to music no matter how removed they may be.

According to Daniel Levitin's *This Is Your Brain on Music: The Science of a Human Obsession*, multiple-trace memory models suggest that music you've listened to is cross-coded with events of the times when you listened to it. That is; music is linked to the events and the events are linked to the music. For me, both before and after music became a more significant part of my life, this theory rings true as certain songs bring to mind specific memories just as random memories elicit songs from specific times. Not surprisingly these connections continue to grow commensurate with my musical awareness and experiences.

Boston, a melodically-tinged hard rock band named for the more famous city northwest of founder-guitarist Tom Scholz's Maynard, Massachusetts hometown, was one of the very first bands I began listening to when I discovered music on a more personal level. Though I had become quite familiar with some of my sister Diane's albums prior to this discovery (a veritable Who's Who of 70s classics by Heart, Peter Frampton, Eagles, Fleetwood Mac, Firefall, and Stevie Wonder among others), Boston was one of the first I could call my own.

It was more than a year after the 1976 release of their debut album and I recall two positives quickly arising from this timing; their follow-up album *Don't Look Back* was soon released (August 1978) and the announcement of a tour was quick to follow. Of course once we received news of the scheduled Spectrum dates, Dan, Paul and I were quick to make plans to go. Having scraped together the money for tickets but having no means by which to get them, we approached Dan's father Jack to assist (though he left this world prematurely in 1984, at the time he was the go-to dad for such things). As expected he came through for us and although the concert was still a few months away, we had one last obstacle to attend to — a ride to the show.

The Spectrum was an award-winning showplace throughout the 70s and 80s and *the* place for concerts in Philadelphia during that time (and later home to the famed Rocky statue shortly after its move from the steps of the Philadelphia Museum of Art). Opening

From The Inside

on September 30, 1967 with the Quaker City Jazz Festival, it subsequently hosted innumerable events in its forty-two active years and, sadly, was shuttered in early 2010 with demolition beginning on November 23. It was the third and final Philadelphia "Sports Complex" arena to close in recent years (although several other local venues have come and gone since the late 1800s). Individual facilities have already been built to host the four home teams; the Eagles (Lincoln Financial Field), Phillies (Citizens Bank Park) and Flyers and 76ers (the Wachovia Center — which sits on the former site of JFK Stadium). As with most arenas around the country gone are the more inspired and appealing names of the past; the current trend giving way to a deluge of corporate sponsorships. In fact, even the venerable Spectrum fell victim to this torrent when the first of three successive bank monikers was attached to its name beginning in 1994. With no further arena needs in Philadelphia, as of this writing an entertainment complex of several retail and dining establishments is being planned for the site.

Just as with Paul's parents, neither Dan's nor mine were willing to allow us to journey unaccompanied into the city, especially to a concert. So Jack stepped up and offered to drive us. Having purchased four tickets; one of them for another friend who, as it turned out couldn't go, and not wanting to simply drop us off only to have to return a few hours later, Jack decided to attend the show with us. Although we were teenagers in every sense of the word, we got along quite well with him and, as such, truly had no concerns being seen in the company of one of the most dreaded and embarrassing of all creatures — a *parent!* Rather, we were quite happy to have been driven door-to-door across the bridge into Philadelphia — and at no cost to us aside from our tickets.

~~~~~

Fun Fact: Boston was playing a two-night stand at the Spectrum on October 30 and 31. In support of his recently released live album *All Night Long,* self-proclaimed "Red Rocker" Sammy Hagar opened the first night's show and Kentucky-based pop-rock band Exile (who would five years later become a successful country band) opened on night two. As our tickets were for the first show, technically the first performer we ever saw in concert was Sammy Hagar.

~~~~~

Soon after Sammy completed his set, Boston took the stage to rousing applause. Immediately upon hearing the opening chords of *Rock & Roll Band* we were rapt; watching, singing and following along in any number of ways to be expected at a concert — especially a *first* one. The darkened arena (or "house" as the interior stage and seating area is more commonly known), vivid light show and oversized pipe organs were more than enough to captivate us. But seeing and hearing so many songs we had come to know by heart being played live by a band that, until then, we had only seen in magazines and on album jackets further enhanced the moment. With the band members *right there* and an overall charge in this new environment, the songs seemed to reach heightened levels of intensity.

Former Guns N' Roses drummer Steven Adler recounts a similar first-concert experience (KISS) in his autobiography, *My Appetite for Destruction: Sex & Drugs & Guns N' Roses*: "The most important thing I took away from the concert was an appreciation for how much the studio version of a song could take on a life of its own when it was performed live. It was the same song, same lyrics, same chord progression, but it was totally different, having a unique and often superior energy all its own."

The next ninety minutes was a blast of music and energy that, although not unexpected, riveted us in new and infinitely exciting ways. By the time the closing chords faded on *Party* and the house lights came up we were far more than just "feelin' satisfied," as lyrics of their song by the same name suggest. We were elated... and hooked.

According to Levitin, "Young children start to show a preference for the music of their culture by age two." But the teen years are when they experience a "turning point for musical preferences" as that's a period of emotionally-charged self-discovery. Further, science has shown an intimate relationship between our memory system and our emotional system and this is why, as adults, we tend to be nostalgic for the music of our youth.

Though we may continue to discover and appreciate new music throughout our lives, studies show the intense physiological connection made during adolescence has our musical tastes fairly well formed by the age of eighteen or twenty.

As Levitin states, "It is around fourteen that the wiring of our musical brains is approaching adult-like levels of completion."

Fun Fact: As I was writing this segment, coincidentally in late October, I received via email an MP3 recording of this very show from an online Boston concert collector. I paused to listen to a few songs as it was my first opportunity to hear them since attending the show almost thirty years ago to the day. As I listened I thought, *"How many people from my generation have a recording of the very first concert they ever attended?"* Now *that* was a rather timely, surreal and perhaps potentially cross-coded moment.

It was obvious that music found its proper place within me and from that point forward it would remain a veritable constant no matter how occasionally intense or relaxed. It would indeed become more deeply cross-coded with many events in my life and, in turn, many events would be equally affected by it.

Sadly, on March 9, 2007 Boston lead vocalist Brad Delp died of an apparent suicide by carbon monoxide poisoning in his home in Atkinson, New Hampshire. He was only fifty-five years old.

FOUR
Front & Center with Cheap Trick

February 21, 1981

Trying is the touchstone to accomplishment
— Paul von Ringelheim

One day in early fall 1978 a middle school friend named John Batz told me that he had seen Cheap Trick at the Spectrum the night before. John was a fellow drummer and around that time had gotten a brand new set of Rogers drums which, to me, were an amazing sight and an incomparable delight to play. Even simple memories of the exhilaration I felt when playing them remain palpable and take me back to the days when music was still newly intoxicating — when that visceral connection was felt for the first time.

The eight-piece kit sounded so full and "professional" and looked equally so with Metallic Sky-Blue shells, brilliant chrome hardware and multiple cymbals. I recall thinking how "cool" it was that they were set up in the center of the family room — actually a second family room separated by a sliding glass door. We would put on headphones, stack albums on the turntable and take turns playing along to songs by Foreigner, Aerosmith and Styx, among others.

Though we were the same age, John had a few years of

experience on me. But that in no way stalled my enthusiasm for playing, even as he watched and listened. Further, because the kit sounded and felt so good, so "right" as I recall thinking, playing it actually made me sense that I was transcending my abilities. And on some level I believe it was that perceived poise which may have contributed to whatever musical development I actually achieved. Whether on John's kit or my own, I simply continued to play; practicing as long and as often as possible. Perhaps I picked up on early lessons about confidence, cause and effect or even mind over matter. All I know is it consumed me at the time and, as one of the most memorable slogans in advertising history would years later urge, I was *Just Doing It.*

Cheap Trick, a melodic yet hard-edged band from Rockford, IL, gained worldwide stardom by way of a successful live album, *Cheap Trick at Budokan,* released in early 1979. With this distinction they joined a narrow category of artists who experienced similar newfound success or reignited popularity by the same means. From Peter Frampton reaching number one on the Billboard charts in 1976 with his double live album *Frampton Comes Alive,* to U2 becoming a hugely popular live band following 1983's *Under a Blood Red Sky*; bands would sometimes and surprisingly find new audiences by way of *albums* with audiences. Even Johnny Cash reestablished himself by way of a live album, albeit with a slight twist on the format, when he released *At Folsom Prison* in 1968. Reaching number one on the country charts, largely on the strength of his 1955 song *Folsom Prison Blues,* it revitalized his career and prompted his 1969 follow-up album *At San Quentin.*

In his self-titled autobiography, Guns N' Roses guitarist Slash (born Saul Hudson) comments on his preference for listening to live releases first when discovering new bands: "I would start with the band's live album, because I believe that is the only way to determine whether or not any band is worth your attention. I still believe that the best representations of my favorite bands were captured on their live albums…"

Though I had not yet gone to my first concert I was a fan of Cheap Trick and therefore very interested in hearing about John's overall experience. As a drummer, though quite new to the role, I was even more curious about the details; how the drums sounded and looked, whether Robin Zander sang as good live as he did on record, if it was loud and so on. I recall John specifically telling me about Bun E. Carlos' drum solo and how at one point he played with an oversized pair of sticks the size of baseball bats. I was fascinated; envisioning each moment as he described it and thinking about how great it must have been to be there.

A few years later when it was announced that Cheap Trick was coming to town in support of their *All Shook Up* album, Dan, our mutual friend Scot Ward and I were immediately interested (this would be *Scot's* first concert). Despite the somewhat unusual pairing at the time of an American pop rock act with a British soft metal band (UFO), as fans of both but having yet to see either we were eager to catch them live. With third-level, last-row seats literally at the wall and as close to the rafters of the Spectrum as you can get, we couldn't have been much farther from the stage. Although it was an interesting panoramic view of the entire house, musically speaking it wasn't preferable from either sight or sound perspectives. All the same I managed to (reluctantly) remain in those seats for UFO's opening set, but decided to seek better viewing options when Cheap Trick took the stage.

Fun Fact: The third-level seating was added several years after the Spectrum's 1967 opening and operations continued throughout the construction phase. The floor's concrete was removed and replaced with dirt so a crane could be brought in for the installation. When concerts were scheduled during this time, all heavy equipment was removed and the floor seats were placed directly on the dirt and gravel.

That neither Dan nor Scot came with me on this first effort at sneaking down to the lower levels was of no concern to me. If truth be told, as I'd discover during many future attempts, even though sharing in these scheming activities can be part of the fun, it's sometimes best just to go it alone so as not to be hindered in any way. And so it was that I surpassed even my own expectations by making my way, unaccompanied, from the farthest reaches of the arena to what are typically considered the best seats in the house. Still, this was not without a few detours along the way.

After being denied access by a few conscientious ushers, with the house lights down I was finally able to slip past one of them amid the chaos of multiple concert goers all bunched up and awaiting the standard flashlight inspection of their tickets. Even though this only got me to the first level it was usually the most difficult area to penetrate; essentially the Checkpoint Charlie of the concert hall beyond which there were no more archway passages, only open aisles and seats grouped in numbered sections on the floor. This success allowed for more freestyle roaming, though no less guarded. Once on the first level additional challenges included jumping the boards, getting to the floor and then meandering ever closer to the stage past more ushers; most of whom were respectably intent on earning their pay. But I managed my way past them and in relatively short order found myself merging into the tightly-packed, standing-room-only mass of humanity that was… the front row. I remember thinking, *"So this is what it's like!"*

Immediately upon settling into place I felt a sense of satisfaction for having successfully navigated my way through the maze of checkpoints and arriving so close to the action. Interestingly, the light show that was so vivid and impressive from afar suddenly became less so as the broad range of colors was seemingly thrown into the audience behind me with only the white light raining down on the first few rows. The stage monitors, or "wedges" in sound-crew vernacular (which are increasingly disappearing in favor of in-ear monitors — or IEMs), were only a few feet beyond my reach, and, as clichéd as it sounds the beads of sweat on the band members' faces were clearly visible. It was almost as if I was onstage with them and seeing all these things from their perspective. Glancing back over my shoulder at the thousands of fans singing along made me wish I actually *was* up there.

This amped-up feeling from being so close to the stage was

not at all an unusual condition as people who attend live events often prefer being closer to the action than farther away. Whether a concert, stage production or sporting event, it's generally agreed upon that closeness seems to add to the level of excitement experienced (and costs commensurately more as well!). And as it turns out this response to proximity may have more to do with our internal wiring than previously known.

Newly discovered brain cells called mirror neurons seem to play a large part in how we perceive and react to the nearness of an occurrence. When a study was done at the University of Tübingen in Germany to test reactions in the brain when a specific action occurred within a subject's peripersonal space — the area within arm's reach — it showed that mirror neurons fired more rapidly than when the action occurred from greater distances. Further, the findings suggest an expanded role for mirror neurons, or "smart cells," in social interaction.

According to *Mirroring People: The New Science of How We Connect with Others* by Marco Iacoboni, Professor of Psychiatry and Biobehavioral Sciences at the University of California at Los Angeles, "Mirror neurons undoubtedly provide, for the first time in history, a plausible neurophysiological explanation for complex forms of social cognition and interaction... and may be encoding actions in a way that's essential for cooperating with others."

Well, I certainly made my way to the front row by "cooperating" with guards (as they looked away) and being there *was* far more exciting than sitting in my third-level seats. So it may be a safe assumption to say that my mirror neurons were working overtime on this night!

As I again turned to face forward, newly-recruited bassist Jon Brant was directly in front of me and I intuitively reached out in typical "shake my hand" fashion. But in lieu of reciprocating, he gave me his bass pick — effectively enhancing my first front-row experience to some degree (an occurrence that was repeated at an October 20, 1982 Van Halen show when guitarist Eddie Van Halen handed me his signature-inscribed guitar pick in that same spot). I suspect that my appreciation was not lost on Jon; given the likelihood that he's done the same thing for other fans during other shows in other towns. Holding fast to my new prize, I took note of its well-worn tip and white-type Cheap Trick logo before slipping it deep into the pocket of my jeans and returning my attention to the stage.

Although I had never before tried to better my seats at a concert, having gone from the third-level "nosebleed" section to the front row — and then to also have been given a memento of the experience — set somewhat of a lofty precedent. But regardless of future successes (or potential failures), I was convinced it would not be the last time I'd at least attempt to get those mirror neurons firing again.

FIVE
Genesis: A New Perspective

August 21, 1982

Adventure is worthwhile in itself
— Amelia Earhart

Until my friend Alex Bojanowski more formally introduced me to their music during the summer of my sophomore year, I was only marginally interested in the British progressive rock band Genesis. Though I knew some of their hits, owned two albums (1976's *Wind & Wuthering* and 1981's *Abacab*) and saw them with Alex at the Spectrum in late 1981 (to no surprise he recently reminded me how I convinced him to follow me from our first-level seats to the floor), at the time I was unfamiliar with the rest of their catalog. As a musician, however, I was well aware of the notable, respected and sometimes changing lineup of Peter Gabriel, Steve Hackett, Phil Collins, Mike Rutherford and Tony Banks as well as longtime touring musicians Daryl Stuermer and Chester Thompson — perhaps one of the more understated and underrated drummers of his time.

Fun Fact: Chester Thompson (born in my birth city of Baltimore, Maryland) has recorded and performed with various artists from the worlds of jazz (Weather Report), rock (Frank Zappa), pop (Genesis) and gospel (Ron Kenoly). He is currently an Adjunct Instructor at Indiana's Belmont University School of Music teaching applied drum lessons and directing a jazz ensemble.

~~~~~

Original Yes drummer Bill Bruford was also one of Genesis' touring musicians when he spent six months on the road with them in 1976 prior to Chester's arrival. Though a relatively short stint, his efforts can be heard on their live albums *Seconds Out* and *Three Sides Live* as well as their video release *Genesis: In Concert*.

In 1982 the band, by now only Phil, Mike and Tony, released *Three Sides Live* — their third live album — which focused heavily on material from the previous two studio releases *Duke* and *Abacab* (the latter title derived from an early arrangement of the musical parts that make up the title track). By then their style had begun to take a decade-long change; less progressive and more pop oriented, and they suddenly found their songs getting plenty of radio airplay while the accompanying videos entered heavy rotation on the still-novel and still-music channel MTV.

An avid fan of music Alex was also quite artistic; the covers of his notebooks reflecting both interests in an array of richly-drawn artist names and band logos. Creedence Clearwater Revival, Little Feat and The Marshall Tucker Band could be found in design alongside Eric Clapton, Molly Hatchet and others; all indicative of his only slightly varied tastes which, for the most part, were unlike mine.

But thanks in part to his stepped-up introduction, where his taste in music intersected with Genesis so, too, did mine. And when it was announced that they'd be coming to JFK that summer, we decided to go.

It was a typical summer day; hot, sunny and for all intents and purposes perfect for an outdoor concert. We arrived in plenty of time to claim a good spot on the field and, given the musical style of the headliner, see what we thought was an interesting choice of opening acts. Local favorite Robert Hazard & the Heroes was followed by A Flock of Seagulls, Blondie and Elvis Costello. Though we watched Robert Hazard and Blondie, we otherwise waited for Genesis by casually wandering around and people watching (admittedly a favorite pastime).

One of the more fascinating people in the crowd was a visibly intoxicated member of the local stage crew, as evident by the gray pass on his shirt. Alone, disheveled and physically unbalanced, he was spewing nonsense to no one in particular. As Alex and I watched somewhat uneasily but equally amused, he incoherently threatened random passers-by — though hardly an intimidating presence in his condition.

After turning away from this sideshow for a few minutes, I lost sight of Alex. A brief compulsory search turned up nothing and I continued undaunted on my sightseeing stroll. When I eventually climbed the bleachers closest to the front in an effort to look into the backstage area (an early and literal attempt to see beyond the façade), I was surprised to see Alex watching the goings-on from a much better vantage point than mine. After a failed attempt to get his attention, I moved on and we eventually reconnected at our spot in the audience, at which point he updated me on the details of his disappearing act.

It turns out that at some point during my moment of diverted attention, Alex approached "drunk-guy" (very uncharacteristic for his typically reserved nature) and simply peeled off the backstage pass that was by then only loosely affixed to his shirt. Applying it to his, he soon found his way to the backstage gate and was granted admission without question. Coincidentally, both he and drunk-guy had long, dirty-blonde hair. And although neither could have been mistaken for the other, Alex could easily have passed for a roadie. And although surprised to learn *how* he acquired the pass, I was just glad that he *did*; knowing full well I'd share in the spoils.

Aside from observing Mike Rutherford engaged in conversation with someone, Alex took a seat on some steps leading to the stage and, from this unique perspective, watched a few minutes of Elvis Costello's performance before being asked by a guard to move. Though he wasn't back there too long on his first visit, he effectively managed to cross that line to the other side and come out grinning. By casually observing the activity and remaining under the radar (albeit with a pass on his chest), he was able to hide in plain view, all but guaranteeing himself no serious challenges by security. During the next hour or two we took turns going back and although I didn't see much of note, I certainly enjoyed my initial taste of being backstage.

After darkness had fallen and Genesis was a few songs into their set, I decided to seize the moment and get a behind-the-scenes look. So I borrowed the pass from Alex, headed for the gate and was soon taking a brief cautionary walk backstage — both to appease concerns about my uninvited status and to become acclimated to this darker version of an area that was awash in sunlight only a short time earlier. When I considered the coast clear enough for my liking, I continued on — regardless how undefined my objective actually was.

After several minutes of listening to the show from behind (not much onstage activity was visible from this ground-level perspective), I took special notice of the left- and right-side ramps leading to the stage. And after the briefest pause to check my surroundings, I began making my way up the left side. Just then a security guard called out to me, flashlight shining, and headed in my direction. I turned to face him, saying nothing but expecting the worst, and he simply shined the light on my pass and said, "You're good," as he turned and walked away. Chalking it up to the Local Crew pass — which allows for onstage access — I breathed a sigh of relief and once again continued on.

I stopped at the top of the ramp and immediately looked out toward the front. The first thing that struck me wasn't that I was onstage with Genesis, but that there were *tens of thousands of fans* in the audience. Though obviously already aware of this, from that unfamiliar vantage point — and as a musician — it was a rather powerful moment that quickly gave me perspective on the amount of pressure a band is under each time they take the stage. Of course, as seasoned veterans they're used to it. Still, it must be an amazing feeling to observe a sea of faces all out there for *you*... and your *music*.

The risks that day were well worth the payoff — and when I came out of that "wow" moment I realized it was a rather cool thing to be up there near Phil Collins' drums, watching Chester Thompson play and standing behind Tony Banks as he played an array of keyboards in his typically composed manner. The show was in high gear as Phil and the others held court front and center and for those few moments onstage my sideline view of it all was amazing. It would be more than two decades before I'd experience — or recreate as it were — a similar feat.

SIX
A Quiet Riot in California

September 21, 1984

Any fool can make a rule and any fool will mind it
— Henry David Thoreau

The first time I actually met any perceived rock stars was when I lived in Sacramento, California while pursuing my own musical dreams. The event was a record signing at, appropriately enough, the very first Tower Records which opened in 1960 on Watt Avenue. Quiet Riot was scheduled to appear there before headlining a show that night at the Cal Expo Amphitheater (with opening acts Kick Axe and Whitesnake). As Scot and I already had our tickets to the show and with the afternoon free, we decided to take in the signing as well.

Upon arriving at Tower the line of fans in front was already snaking down the sidewalk and out into the parking lot. Just as we joined in, the doors opened and the procession began slithering forward toward its rockstar prey.

Although I considered Quiet Riot to be mostly musical "fast food" — a category for bands with a few good songs and hooks but with an overall limited range — I became a fan of their 1983 album

Metal Health when heavy metal was added to my musical palette (although "light metal" might be a more apt description for them). Actually very well received, it was the first heavy-metal album to reach number one on the Billboard charts, bumping The Police's *Synchronicity* from that coveted spot (an album which temporarily ended Michael Jackson's *Thriller* reign — to put it in perspective).

Bearing in mind that their follow up *Condition Critical* had been released only a few months prior, I was a bit hesitant about presenting them with my copy of *Metal Health* as I felt it showed a lack of continued support. But my concern soon diminished when Scot and I finally made it to the checkout counter where the band was situated and each member seemed more than happy to sign anything that was put before them (including several other copies of the same album).

As would later prove true at so many concerts, in these situations I was never one to do things without bending a rule or two — merely in an effort to make it more interesting, of course. So although I handed my camera to Scot to take a picture of me with the band in the background (behind me and across the counter), it became an awkward pose given the circumstances. As a result I promptly took a seat on the counter, essentially mixing in with them, and turned toward Scot for the shot. Store security saw this and immediately tried to usher me down. But guitarist Carlos Cavazzo quickly and kindly waved them off as he and the rest of the band leaned in with me and Scot snapped the picture. Unfortunately that shot came out unrecognizably dark. But other pictures taken of them signing my album and posing with Scot developed slightly better, albeit still quite murky as I never thought to activate the flash feature ("What do you call a drummer with half a brain? Gifted."). Cameras, or lack thereof, would prove to be an ongoing issue in various musical settings in years to come.

It was rather inspiring to have met musicians from a band I was somewhat fond of, yet had only occasionally seen on albums or in videos. And to meet them just hours before they were to take the stage added another layer of excitement to the experience. The concert, which began in the daylight and saw darkness descend by the time Quiet Riot came on, was my first one in California and, as it would turn out, the only time I would see any of those bands live. As such, the entire occasion still holds a unique place in my memory of musical firsts.

Sadly, during this writing it was reported that Quiet Riot vocalist Kevin DuBrow died on November 19, 2007 — only three weeks after his fifty-second birthday — as a result of an accidental cocaine overdose in his home in Las Vegas, Nevada. Regardless of cause, it's always particularly unsettling for me when a fellow musician dies. One of the first artists I ever met, Kevin was the second to subsequently pass away.

Fun Fact: As with all memorabilia I've managed to accumulate over the years, I still have that Quiet Riot album with all my other "vinyl" from the days before music's physical form dwindled from LP record albums to 8-track tapes to cassette tapes to compact discs (CDs) to its current state of digital non-existence. In her autobiography, *Between a Heart and a Rock Place*, Pat Benatar commented about this change and the shift from tape to digital recording: "While I was intrigued by the new process, I was a little freaked out as well. All the tracks, all the vocals, weren't on the twenty-four-track tape; they were numbers stored in air. It was strange to think that there was nothing physical that existed to prove what we'd actually made. It was all just space on a computer." Although the sound of the recordings has improved dramatically with the move to digital, many from my generation and before feel it's unfortunate that album art has been relegated to the size of a CD jewel box. Nevertheless, as they, too, begin falling out of favor — a victim of Internet downloads — the CD-sized art may very well become a welcome sight as the lesser of two evils, aesthetically speaking.

SEVEN
The Mission... and Other Assorted Stuff

Mid 1980s

A wise man will make more opportunities than he finds
— Sir Francis Bacon

Although I had gone to several concerts since seeing Boston in late 1978, by the early 80s I had only sporadic success at digging deeper or obtaining any souvenirs. In reality the notion of actively pursuing those things hadn't yet fully come to mind and, separate of sneaking into better seats at the shows — which became standard practice after Cheap Trick — only occasionally did I try to take it any further. But a few years later following a favorable encounter with a drummer at a 1985 concert, I began creating interactive opportunities a bit more consistently. Knowing it was all in good fun; a victimless crime if you will, I saw no reason not to at least try to pursue it whenever possible. In doing so, by the late 80s I had already met a few musicians, got some autographs and acquired a handful of drumsticks under circumstances as varied as the artists themselves.

That 1985 encounter clearly stirred in me a curiosity about what was possible and an offshoot of my more active involvement in music took hold. The eventual moments of artist interaction, from small local shows to some of the biggest events in music, would soon complement my budding stick collection. And although the meetings were relatively few and far between at the time, as I learned my way around they eventually became more frequent. A variety of guitar picks, setlists and backstage passes would in time be added to my mix of memorabilia and help create what I have come to alliteratively term my mosaic of musical memories.

Whether from major artists in big arenas or a lesser known ones in smaller venues, drumsticks were always the most treasured aspect of these sideline activities as they were a tie to fellow drummers I had admired. From a then-fledgling and fellow New Jersey band Bon Jovi in 1985 to local group Smash Palace (who had just signed with Epic Records) in 1986, if I was into their music I'd try to make that connection no matter how fleeting. It was these initial encounters that would lay the groundwork for what was to come.

But the inspiration to even more vigorously begin collecting sticks didn't hit me until a concert in 2007. In fact my efforts waned for many years as I seldom thought about it at any of the shows I had gone to in the 90s. This was largely due to music having taken a backseat to my personal life. I got married, had children and settled in to the wonderful chaos of family life during that period. As I so often say about the ease with which we can all get sidetracked at various times: "Life takes over." But life's path can sometimes be cyclical and eventually — thankfully — I became musically reconnected both as a fan and an active participant, going to more shows and writing and recording new songs. It was then that the Mission would begin in earnest and my collection would become The Collection, slowly but consistently growing commensurate with my renewed interest in music.

Fun Fact: Just prior to my wedding to Kelley in October 1992, my friend and musical collaborator Kevin Bothwell and I wrote and recorded my wedding song *Just One Moment.* As with keepsakes from other events in my life, I retained the drumsticks used during those recording sessions. They were some of the first Vic Firth sticks I ever bought; their markings sparse compared to their current models: *Vic Firth American Classic Rock.* Although not from some notable drummer admired from afar, they have obvious significant personal value and, as such, I'm quite pleased to still have them.

~~~~~

Though more than twenty-five years have passed since the start of my somewhat unusual hobby, I still seem to remember most of the details surrounding each situation. While recalling the particulars for this book I began to realize there was more to each incident than initially thought. And as the stories began to unfold, a rather fitting twist on an old adage came to mind: "A *drumstick* is worth a thousand words."

••••••••••••••••••••••

EIGHT
REO Speedwagon / Survivor: Making Connections

February 12, 1985

*Appreciation is a wonderful thing;
it makes what is excellent in others belong to us as well*
— *Voltaire*

REO Speedwagon was touring behind their already successful *Wheels Are Turnin'* album in late 1984 when they came to town with opening act and fellow Illinois band Survivor, promoting their most recent release *Vital Signs.*

As usual before shows I was strolling throughout the Spectrum to see whatever I could and to take note of any interesting activity — onstage or otherwise. Less a sightseeing venture than a calculated effort to take the overall concert experience to the next level, my objective was to garner more from the night than merely the intended show. As similar efforts had been moderately successful up until this time, though for the most part limited to sneaking into better seats, I believed Calvin Coolidge's assertion that "nothing in the world can take the place of persistence…" and so set out to put that to the test.

Not long into my walk I noticed Survivor drummer Marc Droubay in plain view on the left side of the stage casually sifting through a box of drumsticks. I watched as he took them out one by one, quickly examined each and then either set them aside or returned them to the box. I assumed those in the latter group were the keepers — sticks with some mileage still left on them. Realizing that nobody seemed to notice him — or perhaps even know who he was — I quickly made my way to the nearest seating section and began speaking with him stage side. In a sort of knee-jerk (perhaps subconscious) reaction, I made him aware that I knew who he was by *telling* him who he was: "You're Marc — the drummer for Survivor." But more importantly (to me at least) I let him know that I was a fellow drummer. Upon hearing this he immediately offered me a used stick, simultaneously tossing one in my direction. Catching it I thanked him and was about to leave when he unexpectedly said, "You may as well have a pair," and tossed another.

Quite pleased to already have a keepsake of the night; my first-ever pair of sticks from a professional drummer, I returned to my seat eager to share the story with Dan as he had gone with me to the concert. I already considered it a great night — and the show had yet to begin.

Although there were plenty of guitar and amplifier endorsements by top guitarists and bassists at the time, there weren't nearly as many for drummers. This was particularly true for drumsticks. As such, Marc's wood-tipped sticks have no indication of his name, the band name or the stick manufacturer — just worn, light blue, stamped notations of wood type, size and country of origin: *Hickory Sticks - P2B - Made In USA*. But official details notwithstanding I know when, where and from whom I got them and that's certification enough for my humble collection.

In my unceasing effort to see what more I could get for my price of admission (apparently a pair of drumsticks wasn't enough for one night), as soon as REO ended their show, I casually began a conversation with a Spectrum security guard by the name of Larry

Jasper. In ice hockey vernacular Larry worked the center-ice door of the boards (actually off-center) which surround the rink and, when topped with protective glass during games, keep fans safe from the danger of airborne hockey pucks. In a concert setting, however, the boards have no glass and merely separate the first-level seating sections from the floor seats. It was at this post where I met Larry, quite unaware that it was actually the backstage entrance. I fully expected that to be, well... much closer to the *stage*.

During my conversation with Larry people would occasionally walk up and he'd opened the door for them, letting them pass into the narrow corridor that led to an area beneath the seats. Seeing the various passes hanging around their necks I quickly realized that this was at least *some* type of behind-the-scenes access. So I asked Larry and he informed me that it was indeed the backstage entrance. A light went off in my head at that moment and thoughts began churning about how I was going to finagle my way in. Within minutes of my discovery I quite candidly, yet politely, asked Larry if he would "let me back." Of course that approach didn't work too well — nor should it have — and additionally it was met with a chuckle; one I would come to know well in the ensuing years. I didn't have the audacity to ask again once refused because even though I was perhaps somewhat bold where these efforts were concerned, I was at least sensible enough to know that pestering a security guard simply was not how to go about achieving my goal.

Instead, I began asking Larry questions about his job and quickly gained a sincere curiosity about all he's seen in his years working concerts. We actually ended up having an enjoyable conversation as he detailed for me a few artists with whom he's had at least peripheral contact. He mentioned the names of some of those who typically stay for after-show meet-and-greets (Van Halen) and which ones, following their performance, leave without much, if any, delay (Billy Joel). Understandably, he seldom came to the Spectrum to see games or shows as he said he always seemed to be working them. Following this brief but engaging exchange it was my assessment that Larry, perhaps in his early-forties at the time, was just an all-around good guy. As such, I was glad to have gotten to know him a bit on that night.

As time passed during our talk the departing audience thinned to almost nobody and I was very nearly about to bid goodnight to Larry with no further mention of going backstage. But presumably sensing that I still had every desire to do so, he looked around as if to see that all was clear and then casually opened the waist-high door between us. Without a single word — only a slight directional nod of his head — he motioned me through. Completely surprised, but wasting no time, I instantly heeded his unspoken words, discreetly thanked him and blindly found my way to the backstage area where others were already assembled and waiting.

I never forgot Larry's kind gesture on that night and would reconnect with him at many shows after that — not always with the intent of getting another free pass (although he certainly came through on more occasions — for Van Halen, Michael Bolton and John Mellencamp, among others). Rather, I would simply stop by his post to say hello and chat with what I considered to be a newfound friend.

Fun Fact: A chance meeting at this show reacquainted me with Kevin, whom I hadn't seen in many years. As we both happened to have tickets in Section W — separated only by approximately ten seats and an aisle — once we recognized each other, small talk ensued over the din of the crowd and within minutes phone numbers were exchanged. Fueled mainly by our mutual interest in music and the seemingly rare discovery that each was still very actively playing, we connected soon after, began writing together almost immediately and eventually formed our band Upper Level. We've been musical collaborators, occasional backstage adventurers and close friends ever since.

The waiting area, as I discovered once there, was essentially a fairly small and non-descript press room. There were a few televisions mounted on the walls and the tables were set up with various brands of beer on ice and some already picked-over finger food; all of which I avoided. Chairs were situated around the perimeter and it was rather well packed with approximately twenty-five to thirty people; some engaged in muted conversations, others waiting quietly in the chairs or simply standing. Scanning the others in the room I noticed that I was the only one without a backstage pass stuck to my shirt. But this was of little concern to me as I knew they served primarily as a right of entry and I was already in. At any rate I kept a low profile and was quite content to make minimal small talk with the others. Leaning against a wall I quietly and calmly awaited the band's arrival.

Within forty-five minutes or so all the members of REO Speedwagon came walking in unannounced and the awaiting fans descended upon them as would be expected — and as the band was likely quite used to. Although I'm not sure how long it took for me to actually get some face time with them amid the throng of admirers; I do recall being patient about it. Standing openly among their fans with no tables or guards to form a buffer in between, the band managed to create a more personal atmosphere. But they remained next to one another in some semblance of a line, which made the interaction easy and orderly. Through it all, as I met and spoke with each of them, I was struck by how engaging they were and how genuinely happy and appreciative they seemed to be in this setting. No discernible signs of self-importance or affectation, just a rock band enthusiastically meeting their fans.

As I've looked back on that encounter (and others like it) more recently, I've come to realize that the band members were only in their mid-thirties at the time — an awareness which gave me pause as I'm now about ten years older than that. I sensed that being professional musicians at that level and at that age — young enough to enjoy it but old enough to respect it — must have been accompanied by a considerable amount of satisfaction (and pride at having earned it).

Wearing a bright red, button-down shirt and having nothing else with me, I figured I'd just have them sign that. As would seem fitting I first approached and introduced myself to drummer Alan Gratzer. When I asked him to sign my shirt he paused and with genuine concern asked, "Are you *sure* you want me to desecrate your shirt just for my autograph?" I assured him it was okay as I simultaneously pulled the fabric taut and he signed. As guitarist Gary Richrath finished signing, he quickly and firmly poked his Sharpie into my left shoulder in a lighthearted effort to put emphasis on the "i" in his name (though as evident by the picture at the top of this chapter, he missed by a mile). He laughingly apologized while patting my shoulder and I shrugged it off in kind before moving on to Kevin Cronin (vocals, guitar, piano), Neal Doughty (keyboards) and Bruce Hall (bass).

Fun Fact: Not knowing if washing the shirt would remove the autographs, I decided simply to include it in my musical memorabilia as is. And although I wouldn't know it until the end of the night, this concert marked two significant firsts for me — my first pair of professional drumsticks and my first true backstage access.

Within approximately twenty minutes of their arrival the band was gone and that part of my night's objective was complete (Coolidge's statement proven!). I headed home with the drumsticks, a shirt full of autographs and some great memories; my first true backstage meet-and-greet experience effectively realized — all thanks to Larry.

NINE
Musical Chairs

When the music changes, so does the dance
— African Proverb

Though this book is primarily about a personal discovery of music and the ensuing events shaped around musicians I've admired and shows I've attended, given its subtitle I would be somewhat remiss not to include a brief history of my *own* experiences playing and creating music as they've always been at the heart of this... thing.

As previously mentioned, not long after meeting Dan in 1977 we discovered a similar interest in music and by the following year simultaneously merged into it more actively; learning to play, writing our first songs and forming our first and often short-lived bands along the way (Unknown Destiny being the one that stands out most from those early days). It was a thrilling time of instruction, both formal and informal, and playing whenever possible simply for the enjoyment of it. In time we began to see — or hear as it were — the fruits of our labors, however modest or unrefined and, our efforts wanting, we continued with hints of progress at various intervals along the way.

Former Yes, King Crimson, Genesis and Earthworks drummer Bill Bruford reflects on the consequence of musical progression in his book, *Bill Bruford: The Autobiography*: "The instrument appears to offer up its delights more readily as it recognizes the hand and touch of an improved player, or perhaps a master."

But despite this gradual advance in instrumental fluency (and the fact that I had saved enough money to upgrade to a beautiful five-piece set of Metallic White Tama Imperialstars — another find in the classified ads) — in time those early songwriting efforts declined, musicians continued to drift in and out and, for me anyway, the enjoyment of playing without a proper band was wearing thin.

As all musicians know playing guitar, drums or any other typical rock'n'roll instrument in high school makes them part of an unofficial club; a self-sustaining word-of-mouth environment where the members all know who one another are — though they may not necessarily know one another. And within this club drummers seem to be even further sorted out as somehow distinct — although not necessarily in a good way. As so many drummer jokes attest, the role of "beating things with sticks" carries with it a dubious assessment of both talent and intelligence ("What do you call someone who hangs out with musicians? A drummer." "What did the drummer get on his SATs? Drool.") — and so on. Though I'm extremely amused by and quick to repeat many of these jokes, this separate classification — at least among drummers — seems to have more to do with camaraderie than anything else.

In *Traveling Music: The Soundtrack to My Life and Times*, Rush drummer and lyricist Neil Peart wrote about this distinction, calling it the "brotherhood of Planet Drum" and referencing how it plays out even among those at the professional level: "Among musicians, it is generally accepted that drummers are 'different,' particularly in their sense of community. Perhaps that is partly a shared humility from being relegated to the 'background' most of the time, and from the lack of respect they were sometimes given by other musicians. The fraternity among drummers was often warm and real…"

In my quest for better playing options, during the next few years I worked with various musicians from this "unofficial club," some from school and others from the neighborhood, eventually forming a trio called Thrust with guitarist Lou Flacche and bassist-vocalist Scott Tretina. We played local parties and various high-school gatherings throughout the year and during the summer. But our finest moment, both in setting and by feat, was undeniably when we took the stage in the 600-seat Shawnee High School auditorium as one of the performers in our sold-out Senior Variety Show. Seeing from my perch on the drum riser a house full of faces packed right up to the foot of the stage; the literal embodiment of the relationship between performer and audience, was, musically speaking, a charge beyond compare for me — before or since. And though we played three songs that night including Led Zeppelin's *Good Times, Bad Times* and Kansas' *Carry On Wayward Son*, my personal highlight was our set-closing performance of Rush's 1978 instrumental *La Villa Strangiato*.

Clocking in at nearly ten minutes and aptly subtitled *An Exercise in Self Indulgence,* the multi-part song is a progression of varying fills, riffs and time signatures — complex enough without any modifications. But as we had also rehearsed — though ultimately chose to pass on playing — another Rush instrumental, *YYZ*; in an effort to validate our efforts I thought to tack on its tritone guitar-bass-drums ending to *La Villa's* abrupt bass-and-drums finish. Likely imperceptible to anyone in the audience other than very discerning Rush fans, it worked out well and satisfied me both from performance and creative perspectives.

Following that show we received quite a few compliments, some about our performance, others about the songs. But perhaps the most meaningful one to me came from Mike Lighthart; a fellow drummer who graduated the year before and whom I had long considered far more accomplished behind the kit than I was. Immediately following our set he met me backstage and in a mix of surprise and expletive-filled enthusiasm said, "Holy shit, dude! I didn't know you were that fucking *good!*" I mention this not out of immodesty, but rather as a testament to how a single statement, in this case of *encouragement*, can resonate within someone and last — perhaps forever. The cautionary side of this story is that the same can just as easily be said for words of *dis*couragement.

In *The Grand Illusion: Love, Lies, and My Life With Styx,* bassist and founding member Chuck Panozzo, details a similar account of encouragement received in 1962 from a nun at his Catholic high school following a negative response from classmates for his band's not-so-great performance: "She said, 'You guys were great. It's just the music you were playing. These kids want to hear rock'n'roll. That's what you need to start playing.' And she was right. It just goes to show the tremendous impact — either for good or bad — that the words of adults can have on young people. If that nun had had a different reaction, I don't know what would have happened to our trio. But we took her words to heart."

Thrust disbanded shortly after the summer parties waned and I found myself making a brief musical go of it in California (as a singer nonetheless — and in two rather divergent bands... the first similar to Ratt, the second U2) before returning to New Jersey, somewhat disillusioned but no less resolute.

Fewer than two years later, coincidentally when I started venturing further into these sideline activities, my musical efforts finally began to more firmly take shape. And as a result of crossed paths, common interests and similar ideas Kevin and I were able to start what would turn out to be the most musically prolific period for either of us; its realization coming in the form of a band we called Upper Level.

Shortly after being reacquainted at that REO Speedwagon show, we met to touch on a few early song ideas beginning with a review of my book of lyrics (in actuality several loose pages). There seemed to be a fairly quick connection and, musically speaking, an agreement on direction. I felt that Kevin's keyboards would be an asset to my writing style and a welcome addition in a band setting. Further, our respective abilities were an obvious complement to one another. In short; my lyrics needed music and his music needed lyrics.

As Peart once stated about the similarly segregated writing method he and his Rush bandmates employ: "It's just a matter of facility really. I have a facility with words that I don't have with notes, and they have it with notes."

Confident something good was happening, I quickly brought

Dan into the fold though we hadn't worked together musically for some time. Soon after, Kevin would recruit bassist Chris Rapkin, whom he had known from high school, and the original Upper Level lineup would be complete. Before long move we'd forward in a creatively fulfilling way… for a time anyway.

Fun Fact: When band names were being considered I suggested Upper Level after discovering those words in black type against a white background on what appeared to be a thin cardboard clothing tag in my parent's home. Not knowing where it came from and never having seen it again, the origin of the tag remains unknown. Once the name was heard, however, it was immediately and unanimously accepted.

Delaware Avenue (now Columbus Boulevard) was home to old, mostly rundown and abandoned warehouses and factories of an uncertain past along the now thriving waterfront section of Philadelphia. It was also home to 1020 RPM Studios; one of very few rehearsal places in the area at the time. The somewhat harsh surroundings and slight edge of threat seemed to add an element of encouragement to our cause and after several months of writing and rehearsing in the various fourth-floor studios we had a handful of songs to our name; mostly up-tempo rockers that hinted at local influences and fell right in line with the music and the sound Kevin and I were aiming for from the start. In fact, the first set of lyrics we reviewed during that initial meeting became one of the first songs we'd complete as a band (*I'll Be Back Tomorrow*). For me this early and productive period was a welcome change from nearly all previous attempts at creating music.

But as so often happens with bands, we soon experienced some personnel changes. First when Chris decided to return to school in Arizona and later when Dan and I had a slight falling out. As bands are commonly compared to marriages due to the closeness and amount of time the members spend together, suffice it to say our split was a result of irreconcilable differences. But thankfully our conflicting views were only related to how we worked together musically. Once that element was removed and some time had passed (nearly two years), the collateral damage of bruised egos healed and a fractured friendship was restored.

By early 1986 both vacancies were filled in bassist Mario DeStefano and guitarist Mario Griati, both capable musicians that brought with them intensity, a desire to write and an unexpected windfall — a private rehearsal space. Situated in a working-class Trenton, New Jersey neighborhood the stand-alone garage-turned-studio was another step forward in the progress of the band and we spent the next few months rearranging current songs, writing new material and playing the occasional show — to include a recorded performance at the nearly empty City Gardens, then one of Trenton's foremost rock clubs. Though this incarnation of Upper Level seemed both creative *and* cohesive the tide would once again turn, changing the landscape of the band; this time permanently.

Seemingly out of the blue Mario DeStefano announced he wanted to leave Upper Level — most surprisingly to form a cover band. Which, given my ongoing drive to be more — not less — creative, seemed like a move in the wrong direction. And though there was no convincing him otherwise, we were at least successful in getting him to work with us long enough to record everything we had completed up to that time. Three weeks after that Labor Day weekend City Gardens show we began laying down tracks for the ten songs we wrote. And in various sessions of recording and mixing, we completed the entire project by mid-October. Not happy with the original mix, which was somewhat rushed in Mario's effort to move on to his new venture, Kevin and I made a "midnight run" to the studio to surreptitiously remix the entire recording more to our liking. Once mixing was complete we left the studio — literally and figuratively closing the door on yet another chapter in the Upper Level narrative.

Mario recruited me as the drummer for his new band Double Standard immediately following the disbanding of Upper Level. And though I was apprehensive at first — again, wanting to move *forward* creatively — he told me about the singer he had lined up and I thought it would be an interesting change of scenery and sound (I also realized just how apt the new band's name suddenly was, given my change of heart).

Karen was the first female vocalist I ever worked with musically and, as such, was the main reason I agreed to join. This new experience quickly turned out to be both enjoyable and rewarding as we moved into territory otherwise off-limits to bands with a male singer. Concentrating on the music of female artists such as Pat Benatar, Heart, 'Til Tuesday, Eurythmics and even Tina Marie; material I had never before played with a band, stirred in me an excitement more typically reserved for *creating* music. Working well together for nearly a year we played some small local shows in the Trenton area, even winning the top prize of $500 in a Battle of the Bands contest at Mercer County College. But in late 1987, when covering other bands' material once again reached that inevitable limit for me, I decided to move on.

In 2003 I learned that Mario had passed away five years earlier following a long battle with leukemia. Equally surprised and saddened by this news I immediately found myself reflecting on our many shared moments as bandmates; even more thankful that Kevin and I urged him to record with us before his departure. Listening to that Upper Level recording once again, my ear was specifically tuned in to his bass lines. And I smiled upon hearing him speak between songs on the recording of that City Gardens show. His passing would be the most unfortunate, unwelcome and hopefully last-of-its-kind addition to my list of firsts. Mario was only thirty years old.

A few years later in mid 1990 I joined another cover band, Midnite Runner, and we spent the next year primarily as the house band for a small South Jersey bar. Although we wrote one or two songs at my urging during that time, a collective interest in becoming an original band was lacking and, as such, by late 1991 I made a decision to uproot. It was an amicable split that ended with me staying on until a suitable replacement was found. When that time came, we hosted one final private show on October 18 at The Hideout, at the time a local restaurant and club that hosted a variety of bands. It has long-since changed to Prospectors; primarily a showcase club for up-and-coming and fairly-well-established country artists.

When Kelley and I were engaged in late January 1992 I immediately and eagerly set out to write our wedding song; a project I considered to be of great personal significance — as well as a challenge to my abilities. And when the line "Just one moment in time turned my life around" came to me while writing one day, it turned out to be the catalyst — and the opening lyric — for the song I aptly titled *Just One Moment*.

Once the lyrics and arrangement were complete, I enlisted Kevin to help bring the music in my head to life. And just as in those early Upper Level days, we once again found "the music and the sound."

Quickly recruiting friend-of-a-friend guitarist Aldo Donato and bassist Clem DaVinci, I booked time at The Music Place Studios in Berlin, New Jersey where we worked on finalizing the song while simultaneously beginning the recording process. After twelve hours in the studio during the course of two days, we completed recording only one week before my wedding.

The work during those recording sessions would be my last active and collaborative playing for nearly a year. But that's not to say I set down my sticks or put my pen in the drawer. On the contrary I maintained a fairly active, though quiet (as quiet as drums can be anyway) musical life at home during that initial year of marriage. Less a choice, it was more a need to continue playing, writing... *creating*. And as the songs and lyrics seemed to be surfacing somewhat as effortlessly as during those early days with Upper Level, I continued capturing them knowing I would — sooner than later — require an outlet for their development.

Bruford affirmed these circumstances rather straightforwardly in *The Autobiography*: "If you have ideas, you need an outlet, or sooner or later you're going to blow up. Depending on others to provide the outlet can be more unnerving than just doing the job yourself."

One year later in October 1993, in need of that inevitable outlet, I reassembled the same group of musicians to record a handful of songs I had written or completed during the previous twelve months, including a remake of Upper Level's *Does She Know*; originally part of that 1986 recording session. Once again Kevin's collaborative assistance was invaluable and with further input from Aldo we completed the project in June 1994. The resulting songs were arranged together on a disc with *Just One Moment* and titled *the Upper Level project — anyway...* in a nod to our former band.

Since then I've continued playing drums, tinkering on guitar and writing lyrics. And more recently and quietly I've even begun a slow-paced solo writing and recording project with Scot Sax, an accomplished Grammy-winning singer, songwriter and founder of Songlife Studios in Ardmore, Pennsylvania. Working outside the confines of a band but with guidance from someone of Scot's caliber, it's my hope that I'll be able to see these newer songs through to fruition — my ultimate goal being to complete another creatively-satisfying musical chapter in my life.

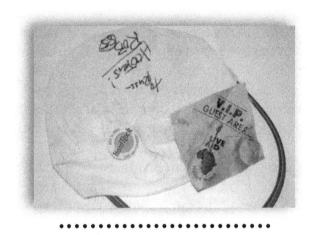

TEN
Live Aid: History in the Making

July 13, 1985

This is your Woodstock and it's long overdue
— Joan Baez

Perhaps the most memorable concert I ever attended — certainly the largest in terms of number of bands and global reach — was Live Aid. Quite notably and specifically intended to raise awareness about and, ideally, help eradicate starvation in Africa, to date it's considered the most successful charity concert of all time and was nothing if not huge. Approximately 160,000 fans attended three simultaneous concerts in the United States, the United Kingdom and Australia (smaller shows were held in other countries) and the sixteen-hour event held on July 13, 1985 was the first ever to be linked by satellite, reaching approximately 1.5 billion people in more than sixty countries worldwide. By the end of 1985 it was said to have generated nearly eighty million dollars for Ethiopian famine relief and countless millions more in the twenty-four years since.

Though Philadelphia's JFK Stadium was rated for a capacity

crowd of 75,000 with its bleacher-style stands and festival seating on the field, Kevin and I were two of the nearly 90,000 fans said to have been in attendance (though reports have suggested that upwards of 120,000 people passed through the turnstiles that day). It was an interesting pairing that would set off a chain of events with Kevin as a pseudo partner in crime to more than a few of my future musical exploits.

Although I became increasingly aware of the show in the weeks prior, I never made an effort to obtain tickets. Perhaps in contrast to the more typical twelve-dollar cost of a concert ticket at the time, the "princely" sum of thirty-five dollars (only slightly more than service charges on concert tickets today) was too much for my budget. Or maybe it was simply that nobody I knew was interested in going. Either way I didn't get tickets and apparently had no plans to go. In hindsight, had I missed this show — more of an event really — it would have left a rather significant void in my collection of musical highlights. But thankfully Kevin *did* make the effort, his creative approach eventually paying off for both of us.

Fun Fact: JFK Stadium was originally named Sesquicentennial Stadium in April 1926 when it was built as part of the Sesquicentennial International Exposition celebrating the 150th anniversary of the signing of the Declaration of Independence. Following the Exposition's closing ceremonies six months later it was renamed Philadelphia Municipal Stadium. But in 1964, in honor of the 35th President of the United States who had been assassinated the year before, it was renamed John F. Kennedy Stadium. On July 13, 1989, exactly four years to the day after Live Aid, JFK Stadium, which had played host to several heavyweight boxing title fights, forty-two annual Army-Navy football games and countless concerts and other events in its sixty-three years, was condemned by Philadelphia Mayor Wilson Goode. The final public event held there was a Grateful Dead concert only six days prior.

Working full time in an office during summer break from college, Kevin was able to call for tickets. As this obviously predated the Internet (and handheld cell phones), tickets for most events had to be purchased at the venue, at a Ticketron ticket office or by phone. I recall many cold mornings spent in line with friends outside department-store Ticketron locations waiting for them to open and hoping we were early enough to get good seats. But always keenly aware that this same scene was playing out at countless locations throughout the area kept my optimism at bay. As it turned out we never once got great seats for any of the numerous concerts we attended throughout the years. But at least we *did* get tickets; and getting in was the primary goal — at least initially.

Armed with his father's credit card and an office phone, Kevin set out to purchase tickets as soon as they became available. After nearly an hour of getting busy signals or being placed on hold for extended periods, an idea came to him. Given that the show was an east coast event local to the tri-state area surrounding the venue, he figured few people would be calling from the Midwest and thus those phone lines would likely not be busy. After getting a Nebraska Ticketron number from information and placing the call, his theory was quickly confirmed. Only moments later two tickets were on their way and he was set to attend what would become one of the biggest concerts in music history.

Fun Fact: July 13, 1985 was officially recognized as "Live Aid Day" in a Joint Resolution by the 99th Congress of the United States. In the document signed and approved by President Ronald Reagan on July 17, 1985, it states among other things: "The President is authorized and requested to issue a proclamation calling upon the people of the United States to observe such day with appropriate programs and activities." Ironically, on the day of the concerts President Reagan underwent scheduled intestinal surgery and from 11:32AM until 7:22PM Eastern Standard Time (EST), Vice President George H. W. Bush was sworn in as Acting President of the United States.

Although the second ticket was not intended for me, in fact Kevin didn't have anyone in mind when he bought it, the offer was soon made and I immediately and gladly accepted. This, he recently stated, turned out to be the "right" choice as I convinced him to stay until the end (11:00PM) despite his apparent readiness to leave sometime in the eight o'clock hour when the long day finally caught up with him. That I also took things to another level later in the evening seemed to provide a second wind that carried both of us to the end and beyond. After all, it *was* another concert and, as such, another opportunity to see what more we could get out of it.

Living across the river in New Jersey at the time, I decided to stay at Kevin's Philadelphia apartment on the corner of 41st & Sansom Streets the night before — about a ten-minute drive to JFK — in an effort to get an early start on the day. With a quick breakfast stop at McDonald's the following morning, we were soon heading to the stadium for what was to become one of our more unforgettable concert experiences. Upon arriving at approximately 6:30AM the crowd was already in full force; thousands of fans milling about the entrances and eager for the doors to open at 7:00AM as per the tickets. After parking Kevin's car, we found the nearest entrance and joined the masses as they headed in. Quickly making our way to the field, completely disregarding the Section EE, Row 48 reserved seating noted on our tickets; we got as close as possible; staking out a spot only about twenty rows back and in front of the MTV broadcast station on the left flank of the stage. The next two hours were spent watching a sea of faces file in all around us as the early morning summer sun began to peak over the uppermost eastern rim of the stadium, its warmth giving us a mere taste of what was to come.

The first person to take the stage was the late legendary concert promoter Bill Graham who introduced the day's first host, actor Jack Nicholson, who, in turn, introduced the day's first official performer, Joan Baez. Before singing *Amazing Grace* Baez announced to rousing applause, "Good morning children of the 80s, this is your Woodstock and it's long overdue!" With those words the concert seemed to be officially underway. Only a few moments later last-minute addition and hometown favorite The Hooters took the stage, injecting a bit of energy into the crowd and waking them up with *And We Danced,* their first single from that summer's major-label debut *Nervous Night*. From that point forward Kevin and I soaked up everything the day had to offer. And although there was no way of knowing it at the time, we would eventually get to see things from slightly more interesting perspective.

Though it was satisfying enough just to have been at Live Aid; essentially the center of the music world on that day, given the scale of the event and the number of artists on hand, it wasn't long before I was thinking about ways to infiltrate the fortress. Occasionally drifting among the crowd to people-watch I found my attention being equally divided between the acts *onstage* and any potential opportunities to get *backstage*. The first prospect was rather obvious and, as such, I knew it was equally unlikely to be successful. But I sided with the old proverb: "Nothing ventured, nothing gained."

The "prospect" was a tall gate to the left of the stage (the same one used for backstage access during the Genesis show) and not far from where we had pitched our proverbial tent earlier that morning. I approached a guard as he was peering over the top into the audience and began making small talk. His occasional opening of the gate for anyone coming or going inadvertently gave me a few opportunities to glance into the backstage area, though I saw nothing of note. Realizing rather quickly that this was a dead end, I retreated into the crowd where I happened to see Bruce Johnston of the Beach Boys. Nobody seemed to notice who he was, perhaps because he was an "older" gentleman in his forties amid a crowd of mostly teens and twenty-somethings. Although immediately recognizable to me, I didn't approach him. Instead I watched as he viewed the stage with an apparent interest in the audience's perspective. Soon after, he disappeared behind the gate only to resurface with the Beach Boys when they took the stage late in the noon hour.

Later, I crossed paths with someone appearing only slightly older than the average audience member. He had a notepad in one hand, a pen in the other and a lime-green, stick-on backstage pass on his shirt that read *V.I.P Guest Area - Live Aid - Feed the World*. Quickly striking up a conversation with him, I learned that he was a reporter for the *Wall Street Journal* — not a newspaper I expected to be covering such an event. And in somewhat of a role reversal, I began interviewing him about his opinion of the show so far, whether he had seen anything interesting backstage, how long he planned to stay and so on. He was actually quite receptive and after a few minutes I thanked him for his time and we parted ways.

When I ran into him again several hours later I noticed he had a larger laminated pass around his neck in addition to the green one. My immediate assessment was that one of them was clearly unnecessary. So, shortly into our renewed conversation I saw an opportunity to act on my theory and eased into it by asking if there was a difference between the two passes. He replied that the laminated one was arranged for him by the *Wall Street Journal* and allowed him more access to do his job. I agreed that this made sense and on the tail end of my reply warily reached out, lightly tugging on a loose corner of the green pass while saying, "… then I guess you won't be needing *this* one anymore." As I slowly, somewhat hesitantly peeled it off his shirt, he seemed surprisingly ill-concerned; actually shrugging it off and allowing me to keep it. Though I contained my excitement at the prospect of what this little pass meant, I thanked him generously.

The potential to get backstage was one thing. But getting a backstage *pass* was far more than anticipated — especially at a show of this magnitude. We spoke for another minute or so, I thanked him once more and again we went our separate ways. When I found Kevin and shared the good news with him, it all looked very promising. But when I actually shared the *pass* with him, well that was a different story.

I was first to take advantage of our newly acquired — albeit illegitimate — status as V.I.P. guests. After changing into more comfortable clothes in the relatively nicer (though not by much) and slightly more spacious backstage bathroom, I was soon casually walking around and getting a more in-depth look behind the scenes. Among the temporary settings for artists and guests was a Hard Rock

Café arranged under a huge tent, a larger area with sofas, tables and chairs spread out on indoor-outdoor carpet and an open-air section where the summer sun was as unforgiving as it was in front of the stage. A makeshift community of turquoise-green trailers offered a more private respite for artists whose names were clearly marked on the outside of each. And although I did see some musicians, The Cars' guitarist Elliot Easton, bassist Ben Orr and drummer David Robinson as well as Duran Duran bassist John Taylor and Simple Minds singer Jim Kerr, far more prevalent were the event staff, management and Philadelphia police officers manning the show from behind.

Their presence notwithstanding, with my pass firmly affixed to my shirt (I kept checking to make sure it was still on) I strolled around with a degree of reverential confidence, less concerned with being noticed as a gate crasher and more tuned in to the sights and sounds around me. Despite these myriad but welcome distractions, perhaps the most enticing thing I saw that afternoon was the stage-right entrance ramp. It was an inviting opportunity just lying in wait, a chance to be *on* the Live Aid stage — or at least on the stage right flank. But erring on the side of caution, I quickly dismissed temptation and instead headed in the opposite direction to bestow V.I.P. status upon Kevin. After catching up with him in the crowd and offering a quick overview of my exploits, I handed over the pass and off he went to see it all for himself.

After a short time backstage doing most of the same things I did, he came back out via the narrow passage where we both entered. But instead of eagerly approaching with stories from his journey, upon seeing him I noticed an unexpected discontented look; his hands palms-up and out to his sides in what I read as an unofficial but universal sign of speechless yet quizzical confusion. Once within earshot he told me what I'm certain he dreaded having to tell me — that he lost our pass. Just like that our V.I.P. status appeared to have been unfortunately, unintentionally and inextricably revoked. Although my immediate reaction was one of disappointment, my second-nature response was to find another way in. Time was of the essence and so I immediately set off in the direction of the guard at the entryway.

Upon approach I went into small-talk mode in an effort to warm him up to me and, more importantly, to remind him that I was one of the people who had "rightfully" recently passed through his post. I further explained that I must have lost my pass backstage and needed to go back in an effort to find it. Though hesitant at first and not sure what to believe, he seemed to recall letting me back. Pointing to Kevin nearby, I told him I had no intention of ditching my friend to spend the rest of the show backstage. I simply wanted to get my pass and come back out. After a minute or two he acquiesced, allowing me through.

Once in I began an ultimately fruitless search, having taken Kevin's lead that he was in the bathroom just before coming back out. Our expectation was that it would be there if anywhere. When I realized it was a lost cause I remained backstage with the goal of replacing it however possible and soon found the answer in a group of people heading toward an exit gate. Approaching a man who appeared to be only slightly older than me, I asked if he was leaving and, if so, if he wouldn't mind parting with the pass on his shirt (the same type I originally had). Hardly breaking stride or saying much, he agreed by peeling it off and handing it to me on the spot as I thanked him through a mix of composed surprise and delight.

An old Chinese proverb asserts: "Good luck seldom comes in pairs but bad things never walk alone." Though happy to have refuted the former, I would now be careful not to yield to the latter.

With my new pass safely in hand I made my way back to the entryway where Kevin was waiting at the opposite end. Hanging back I enlisted the help of someone exiting; pointing out Kevin and asking if he wouldn't mind delivering the pass to him. He kindly agreed and we both watched closely from either end. Once backstage, Kevin returned it to me — perhaps at my request under the circumstances — and we set off on a similar undertaking both for his benefit and so we could get back to taking advantage of this once-in-a-lifetime opportunity without further delay or difficulty. In relatively short order, using the same tactic, Kevin approached the father of a family heading toward the opposite exit and asked the same question about his hopefully unwanted pass. He, too, amiably agreed handing it over and thereby unofficially and unknowingly reinstating our illicit status as V.I.P. guests. We were back in business; the old proverb challenged and refuted once again.

During the next few hours we drifted in and out of the backstage area at will; sometimes catching a band live from out front and other times simply moving around to take everything in from all angles. Although essentially with access from about midday until the show's end at approximately 11:00PM, we spent the majority of our time in the audience watching what we came for — the concert. But on the occasions when we went backstage, we had the good fortune to meet a few artists.

Our first encounter was with British hard-rock band Judas Priest sometime after they came offstage and were hanging out in the Hard Rock Café. I first approached vocalist Rob Halford who, despite his heavy-metal onstage persona, was actually quite friendly. At one point I half-heartedly offered to trade earrings with him as he had a small hanging cross I thought was cool (I had a small hoop). But he declined, saying that it was given to him by a good friend (although I suspect he was also wondering — and rightly so — why a total stranger was making such an offer).

With designs on getting a few autographs while there but having nothing for anyone to sign, I decided the promotional painter's cap that was handed out would suffice. And for the first one of the day I took it off, handed it to Rob and he signed it. With the exception of bassist Ian Hill, Kevin and I spoke with and got autographs from the remaining members of the band, guitarists K. K. Downing and Glen Tipton and drummer Dave Holland. I approached Holland at the bar of the Hard Rock Café where he was quietly having a beer and asked how long he had been drumming. He said it had been approximately twenty years and that he enjoyed playing for a living (although that would cease in 2004 when he was sentenced to eight years in jail for the attempted sexual assault of one of his male drum students). But the discussion was brief and after he signed my hat, Kevin and I were once again on the move.

As darkness descended we continued to catch some of the show from out front while periodically returning backstage in a demanding attempt to experience everything — seemingly all at once. The nonstop barrage of people and music on both sides of the fence was both stimulating and distracting. But through it all we maintained an ever-present awareness of our rightful place in this circus. Despite our outward appearance of legitimacy in the form of the backstage passes, we never got so comfortable as to completely let down our guard. And it was perhaps this unremitting caginess that allowed us to blend in and remain undetected for the duration.

In the later hours we would meet a few more artists; the Hooters' Eric Bazilian and Rob Hyman among them. As they were heading toward the exit we briefly introduced ourselves; presenting our hats for a few autographs (Kevin also offered the Live Aid shirt he was wearing) before stepping aside and allowing them to continue on their way. A moment or two later in the same area I noticed Neil Young as he, too, was heading rather swiftly toward the exit. Though we never connected with him; his leaving made me realize that although we were in a strange world of once-in-a-lifetime experiences, the performers were essentially at work and, as such, far less inclined to hang out in this all-too-familiar, after-show environment. Perhaps to many of them, aside from the scale of the event, it was just another day at the office.

Fun Fact: Ironically those of us in attendance at JFK and Wembley were doubtless part of the biggest news event of the day (President Reagan's surgery aside), yet we were completely out of touch with anything outside those walls. Unlike the instant access to all manner of communication at everyone's disposal today, we were essentially an island unto ourselves not knowing, for the most part, how momentous the event really was as it was happening. And whereas promotional materials for such an event today would be innumerable, there were only a few keepsake items available back then — a program, a poster and a few t-shirts.

In one of our more memorable backstage moments that evening, Kevin and I parked ourselves on a sofa in the large lounge area and just settled back to watch all the activity surrounding us. Although a nice respite from the constant running around we'd been doing all day, by no means was it an arbitrary choice of seating. Directly across from us on an identical tan sofa fewer than twenty feet away sat actress and singer Cher in a white Bundeswehr tank top, white pants and flip flops. Tanned and toned with jet black hair and that smile; she looked as good to me as when she was the focus of my first boyhood crush during her time as the sexy half of the Sonny & Cher show in the early 70s. In those days her bare midriff, low-cut tops and exotic blend of Cherokee and Armenian descent were enough to captivate me in an excitingly unfamiliar way. And although that crush had long passed, being in her company some thirteen years later was both exhilarating and a bit nerve-racking.

After approximately twenty minutes of intermittently glancing in her direction and musing about if, when and how we should approach her (Kevin said I intended to somehow give her a kiss — though I don't recall that claim I don't doubt it either), we finally stood up and walked around to the back of her sofa. Literally with hat in hand I extended my painter's cap asking for an autograph while immediately following up with a compliment surely and subconsciously long held over from those boyhood crush days; "I think you're beautiful." Ugh. It was as spontaneous and sincere as it was nauseatingly sycophantic. But once words are spoken there's no way of taking them back — and I suppose I didn't really want that anyway. Regardless — and thankfully — she took it as intended while smiling and offering a semi-embarrassed (or perhaps equally nauseated); "Thank you, that's really sweet." As she handed back the hat I could do little more than thank her, shake her hand and sheepishly walk away. Kevin, not nearly as taken with her as I was, once again offered the shirt on his back as the canvas for yet another autograph and she happily obliged.

Although the entire day was filled with a veritable Who's Who of rock music's elite, the later hours seemed held in reserve for some of the biggest performers on both sides of the Atlantic. With The Who, Elton John and Paul McCartney at Wembley and Eric Clapton, Phil Collins and Led Zeppelin at JFK; the evening seemed rife with veteran talent — all notably British — and designed to bring this already remarkable show to a suitably pleasing crescendo.

Fun Fact: The highlight of Live Aid may very well have been the self-arranged reunion of the three remaining members of the legendary Led Zeppelin — singer Robert Plant, guitarist Jimmy Page and bassist John Paul Jones (although Phil Collins is often noted as covering on drums for the late John Bonham, Chic and Power Station drummer Tony Thompson, who died in 2003 only two months after the passing of fellow Power Station singer Robert Palmer, also played alongside Collins during Led Zeppelin's set). At the time both Robert and Jimmy were touring America individually — Robert behind his recently released third album *Shaken 'n' Stirred* and Jimmy with his latest band The Firm — while John was back home in England. When Robert volunteered to take part in the benefit concert, promoters paired him with Eric Clapton. But he nixed that in favor of calling on Jimmy who agreed to the arrangement. Together they reached out to John who responded, "Well, if you're gonna do a Zeppelin number, I know a Zeppelin bass player."

Not least among these veterans was one of the more eagerly awaited artists on the bill — Mick Jagger — who performed both solo and in a duet with Tina Turner. In a testament to his elevated status in the hierarchy of rock'n'roll, Mick was followed only by Bob Dylan who, interestingly, performed with Mick's Rolling Stones band mates Keith Richards and Ron Wood during an acoustic set of some of his classics.

Milling about backstage when Mick came on, Kevin and I soon found our way to the televisions set up in the Hard Rock tent and caught a few minutes of the MTV broadcast of his performance. Admittedly, it was a bit strange and perhaps foolish to be watching on television a rock'n'roll icon of Mick Jagger's stature when we were *at* the show. But under the circumstances it made sense and soon paid off well, albeit fleetingly, for me.

Following his performances Mick exited stage right down a long ramp (the "ramp of temptation" from earlier in the day) with a slightly hurried gait, the requisite towel draped around his neck and his face damp with sweat. As luck would have it I happened to be at the foot of the ramp just then. With a guard standing post, his arms outstretched in an effort to keep the path clear — but with me still in *front* of him — I was certain I'd be told to move. Surprisingly, and perhaps as a result of the slight commotion surrounding the moment, that never happened. So as Mick approached, with one or two handlers in tow, I was directly in his path and within seconds found myself face to face with him. Caught up in the moment I instinctively extended my hand and offered an impulsive, "Hey Mick!" He returned the gesture mid-stride, likely a knee-jerk reaction from countless similar situations, and before I knew it I had shaken hands with one of the biggest names in rock'n'roll.

It was a fairly exciting moment and yet only a few seconds out of a nearly sixteen-hour day of music. But given that it was Mick Jagger, front man for "the world's greatest rock'n'roll band" — or surely the most tenured one — it certainly topped things off in a rather noteworthy way. I recall almost immediately thinking about how my friend Scot, the ultimate Stones fan, would react to this story. *"He's gonna be floored,"* I thought.

He was.

In all probability meeting Mick Jagger would be considered a once-in-a-lifetime occurrence — and that's certainly what I thought following our brief encounter. But only a short time later while the concert's finale was occurring onstage, Kevin and I noticed a white van by a vehicle access at the back of JFK. Along with many others still working or simply lingering about in this deeper recess of the backstage area we began to detect a certain "buzz" in the air around the van. Upon a driver's side approach we suddenly observed Mick and his entourage just as they hopped into the passenger side. Standing directly outside the backseat window, we saw him slide in and were once again face to face, albeit separated by glass.

The van doors quickly closed and the driver began slowly pulling away when he was suddenly signaled to stop. Someone, presumably from a Live Aid public relations team or some similar group, relayed a message to the van and within a moment, just as quickly as he got in, Mick got out.

Approximately twenty-five feet away sat two identical brand new white Chevy Camaro IROC-Z sports cars that we hadn't noticed before. But given that they were covered with multi-colored autographs from many of the artists present that day, it was apparent they'd been there throughout the show. We later discovered they were to be auctioned off with the proceeds further assisting the Live Aid famine relief cause.

Immediately upon exiting the van Mick headed straight to the Camaros in yet another hurried gait. I shadowed him during this walk (again nobody buffering my approach) while extending a pen and paper and simultaneously asking for an autograph. But my request was not only rebuffed, it was completely ignored. Arriving at the cars he signed each with a different color marker and, when finished, turned and made an equally hasty retreat to the van. Undeterred I followed him back repeating my request and, in one final and desperate plea, stated the unimpressive truth that it was "for my friend Scot in California — he's a *huge* fan." Apparently unmoved and equally undeterred he maintained his focus, hopped back into the van and made a successful getaway, thus ending the day in an almost scripted manner.

However weird and wonderful the circumstances of the day, luck seemed to favor us at every turn and, coupled with our efforts to see and do more, helped make it much better than it otherwise would have been. Whereas most people I've asked remember very clearly where they were during Live Aid, I'm always told that having been there must have been far more exciting. I invariably agree — knowing full well they don't know the *half* of it.

ELEVEN
2nd Annual MTV Video Music Awards

September 13, 1985

Ladies and gentlemen, rock'n'roll
— John Lack

It was with those words on August 1, 1981 that a new cable channel was launched ushering in a new era of entertainment with the marriage of two driving forces in American culture — television and music. Revolutionizing the latter with a play-on-words pronouncement that we'd "never look at music the same away again," its popularity would spawn countless similar formats the world over. Regard for its content prompted an equally popular yearly awards show which celebrated and validated its influence on everything from mainstream media to Main Street America, producing a subset of late 20th-century youth along the way. This legion of post baby boomers born under the banner Generation X would eventually come to be known as... the MTV Generation.

Although Music Television (MTV) — then an all music-video format — already had more than four years behind it, its self-titled awards show, which was held in Manhattan, was still very much in its infancy. But with the channel's mass appeal a similar wave of success soon washed over the show and Kevin and I decided, without much deliberation, to see firsthand what all the excitement was about. Setting out on a journey that would take us nearly ninety miles north into New York City, exactly two months to the day after Live Aid we arrived at the world-renowned Radio City Music Hall for the 2nd Annual MTV Video Music Awards.

Arriving after dark and as the show was nearing its end, we joined the large crowd gathered outside hoping, along with everyone else, to catch a glimpse of a favorite band or artist. Seeing The Tubes' singer Fee Waybill interviewed by MTV VJ Alan Hunter atop a large media truck was one such glimpse — and moments like that were at least one reason why we made the trek. But as always, with no intention of following any sort of protocol and with higher hopes than merely a distant fleeting look here and there, we soon moved "far from the madding crowd."

The entire area at 6th Avenue (Avenue of the Americas) and West 50th Street was as bright as day from the myriad spotlights, streetlights and the ever-present red-neon glow of the block-long, ten-story-high Radio City Music Hall marquee. Wooden police barricades lined the sidewalks and velvet ropes ran the length of the red carpet from 6th Avenue to the Hall's main entrance as hundreds of fans awaited any sign of their favorite musicians.

~~~~~

Fun Fact: The site of Radio City Music Hall was initially planned as the new home for the Metropolitan Opera. But following the stock market crash of 1929 the opera company withdrew from the project. Eventually opening in 1932 as part of midtown Manhattan's twelve-acre Rockefeller Center complex, Radio City derived its name from one of the complex's first tenants; the Radio Corporation of America — more commonly known as RCA.

~~~~~

Still high from our Live Aid excursion, an elevated sense of assurance may have subconsciously had us believing we could replicate that success on some level. In our typically casual yet timeless look of jeans, t-shirt and jacket we certainly looked "Bryan Adams" enough to fit right in and, perhaps with an air of idealistic confidence, tried to do just that when we otherwise had no right — or invitation — to do so. Later on, that moment would remind me of a line from Rush's 1978 song *Circumstances*: "Innocence gave me confidence to go up against reality" — obviously no matter how ill-considered.

After some cajoling, the otherwise reserved Kevin agreed to walk with me up the red carpet in a hail of light, past the throngs of fans, to see what would happen (as it turns out, not much). When asked at the door if we had our invitations we could do little more than stare; at an apparent loss for even a hint of ingenuity. And just like that our misguided effort at an easy entry was dashed leaving us only one option; to go back the way we came. But this return, a walk of shame as it were, wasn't as dreadful as anticipated and only a few moments later would prove a blessing in disguise.

While heading east along the comparatively darker 50th Street side of Radio City, two gentlemen heading in our direction gradually came into view and we immediately recognized one of them as Stewart Copeland, drummer and founder of the British rock trio The Police. Caught off guard I could only put forward a stunned, "Stewart Copeland!" Though first appearing surprised, perhaps at being recognized on this dark side street ("Hey…?"), he graciously indulged Kevin and me as we seized the moment for a quick handshake and a split second with this musician we've both long admired. And though we were deliberately — almost politely — quick to make our introductions and leave him on his way, after eight years in the spotlight by this time he was surely used to this type of random recognition — some of which I would assume has been far more intrusive and belabored.

In his autobiography, *Strange Things Happen: A Life with The Police, Polo, and Pygmies,* Copeland describes this phenomenon as somewhat of a necessary evil in his line of work: "It may have been inconvenient, but this is what I had come for. Notoriety is an odd by-product of music but essential. The music transports the musician himself first of all but bewitching others is really what it's about. Music is an amplifier of one's self. If it doesn't capture attention, then the magic is sterile. So being stared at is part of the deal, and at first it was just fine to create a stir just by existing."

Our encounter, both brief and memorable, was brought into being by chance and it would once again be chance that favored us in the form of good timing when, soon after, we managed our ultimate goal on the night — entry into the legendary and venerable Radio City Music Hall.

As an older couple exited out a side door onto 50th Street, I immediately and politely held the door for them — though my courtesy was not without ulterior motive. And once they walked out, we simply walked in having no idea where this entrance would take us — which, of course, was immaterial. Finding ourselves in a large reception area just outside the main concert hall and feeling a bit out of place, we quickly made our way even further inside to find that the house was nearly empty; the show having obviously ended.

Fun Fact: Prior to 2002 the MTV Video Music Awards show was traditionally held on the second Thursday of September. That date has since been moved back one week so as to never coincide with the anniversary of the September 11, 2001 terrorist attacks.

Essentially having free reign of the empty hall we made our way toward the front and along the way found show programs left on seats by attendees (I believe mine to have been Julian Lennon's as evident by a tape of the show I saw the following day). Climbing a set of stairs leading to the stage we were soon behind the curtain and standing in front of an unattended table full of MTV "Moon Man" awards. Perhaps distracted by the moment I avoided them. But Kevin actually picked one up, giving at least a flash of thought to keeping it. He quickly thought better of that, however, and placed it back on the table as we continued on through the back halls of Radio City.

Having no idea what was around each corner, where we'd end up or even what we'd do once we arrived, we were just living in the moment. The excitement of the unfamiliar, the appeal of the unknown and the prospect that no matter what it was, it would surely be better than standing outside among the crowd was, in and of itself, worth any effort we had made to get there.

It was on this leg of our maze-like journey that Kevin discovered a white sign with an MTV logo and the words "To Press Room" on it. This time he wisely seized the opportunity for a souvenir, immediately taking it off the wall, rolling it up and keeping it. Nearly twenty years later, still in great condition — albeit yellowed from the passage of time — he made a copy for me and I randomly placed more than fifty of my concert tickets around the perimeter, framed it and hung it as a centerpiece of sorts directly behind the drums in my music room. Aside from its distinctiveness, to me it serves as a great reminder of one of the best summers on personal record.

Eventually catching up to some voices we heard somewhere ahead of us, we began following them as they made their way to a stairwell which led to yet another unknown destination (to us anyway). Upon sight we realized they weren't just other people, but rather some members of two prominent Boston bands from the time, both of whom were up for awards on this night; The Cars and 'Til Tuesday. During our ascent, Kevin and I quietly wondered how we might approach them for an impromptu meet-and-greet. But before we knew it, a moment of serendipity provided the opportunity for us.

Arriving at the top, at street level as it turned out, we discovered the door to be locked leaving us all stuck in the stairwell. As the only two "civilians" in the mix, Kevin and I engaged in some small talk with our fellow captives; The Cars' Ben Orr (bass, vocals) and Elliott Easton (guitar) and 'Til Tuesday's Aimee Mann (bass, vocals), Robert Holmes (guitar) and Joey Pesce (keyboards). As everyone made light of the situation, I sought 'Til Tuesday's autographs for my show program as Kevin mentioned to Ben Orr that The Cars was the first band he had ever seen in concert. Ben was quick with a tongue-in-cheek reply; "So, we brought you up *right*!" Following Kevin for The Cars' autographs, I simply handed my program to Elliott casually saying, "Ditto" (sign mine also). He, too, was lighthearted about the moment, "Okay, Ditto," as he proceeded to sign accordingly: *"To Ditto — Elliott Easton."*

Sadly, in April 2000, it was announced that Ben was diagnosed with pancreatic cancer. He passed away later that year on October 3 and would be the first musician I met to have died. Ben was only fifty-three years old.

Eventually someone opened the door from the other side and our up-close-and-personal time with the bands was over. But just as quickly a new set of circumstances was upon us as we were thrust into a crowded and somewhat chaotic vestibule that appeared to be a standing-room-only departure lounge, an in-between point for the artists as they were called for their limos. The process as we witnessed it was that a limo would pull up and the driver would announce his intended pick-up to a runner. The runner would then go inside and notify the party, whereupon they'd then pass through this vestibule on their way out to the sidewalk and into the awaiting car.

Shortly after arriving here we were told we had to leave but were never fully escorted from the grounds. Rather we were only directed out the door to the sidewalk which was an area cordoned off with more wooden police barricades set up in a cattle-shoot arrangement so the artists could pass unhindered from inside to their waiting limos. Needless to say we didn't go any farther than we were told to and as a result stayed within the protected area. So while a few hundred onlookers watched the artists leaving from a bit of a distance, we took it all in from a much more intimate setting.

Among the performers who breezed past us during this appropriately fanfare-type ending to our night were Bob Geldof, Tina Turner, Sting, Eddie Murphy, Don Henley, David Lee Roth, Bryan Adams, Grace Jones, Eurythmics' Dave Stewart and Annie Lennox, Simple Minds' Jim Kerr, The Pretenders' Chrissie Hynde (Hynde-Kerr at the time), Ah-Ha and Ratt's Stephen Pearcy and the late Robbin Crosby.

According to a well-known phrase adapted from Robert Burns' poem *To a Mouse*: "The best-laid plans of mice and men often go awry." Conversely, perhaps it can equally be stated that the least-planned events of a couple of friends can sometimes turn out quite well.

As noted previously, the summer of 1985 was one of the best on record for Kevin and me primarily with regard to how central music was throughout — and the events shaped on this evening were in no small part why. We just seemed to seize the moment at every turn. And as Kevin was so fond of saying back then: "That's what summer's for."

TWELVE
Bon Jovi: Incoming!

October 12, 1985

There is no substitute for victory
— Douglas MacArthur

On the road to promote *Invasion of Your Privacy* in 1985, Ratt had Bon Jovi in the supporting role on the heels of their sophomore release *7800° Fahrenheit*. As the tour made a fall stop at the Spectrum, a few friends and I decided to go as we were fans of both bands. Although I don't recall ever having been lucky enough to have purchased floor seats for *any* of the several concerts I attended back then, that's where I was for the majority of this show.

Fun Fact: Part of my efforts to do and see more at concerts involved sneaking around, jumping over the boards and otherwise maneuvering to get closer to the stage than what my ticket indicated. I was typically alone in these ventures as others were either content to remain in their seats or simply got lost in the shuffle. When someone *would* come with me, it wasn't always successful for both of us. On those occasions when I wasn't the one getting caught, I'd glance over my shoulder only to see my cohort being turned back by an attentive guard. It was always every man for himself in these situations and, as such, I would inevitably press on.

~~~~

Standing in my unofficial floor seat on the aisle during Bon Jovi's performance, I watched as they eventually came to the end of their set. After the final note was struck, the band stepped to the front of the stage for the classic hand-in-hand, wave-and-bow send off. And in customary drummer fashion, Tico Torres took the opportunity to throw his sticks into the crowd. From my perch atop the seat I saw one sailing right in my direction and my focus immediately intensified. Making a perfect arc, it landed in the aisle to my right and I jumped into the instant fray of rabid fans all suddenly competing for this same piece of used lumber. I was shoulder to shoulder with some guy and — as the bodies seemed to continue to pile on top of us — we both had a piece of the stick in our grasp. But after one swift and forceful pull in my direction, I was victorious and in sole possession of "the prize." I emerged from the pile, stick in hand, and the battle was over nearly as quickly as it began.

As with the sticks from Marc in Survivor, Tico's is also wood tipped and quite simple in design with no manufacturer, band or tour noted; only a basic branding of his name and size in small, light blue letters: *Tico Torres - 5B.*

Interestingly, this lack of markings is a good indicator of an older stick's vintage as they rarely had more than a basic printing of name or manufacturer throughout the 70s and into the 80s. But just about all notable drummers today have endorsement deals with stick manufacturers Vic Firth, Pro-Mark, Regal Tip, Vater, Ahead and even cymbal manufacturer Zildjian among other lesser-known brands. And the sticks are personalized in myriad and varied ways to include band names and signatures.

Nearly twenty-five years later Tico's stick is still on display in my collection and he's still behind the kit with Bon Jovi as they continue their impressively long-running career.

THIRTEEN
Local Shots: 1980s Philly

Music is a higher revelation than all wisdom and philosophy
— Ludwig van Beethoven

Philadelphia is a city rich in musical history dating back to colonial times when both religious and secular music was in vogue (though non-religious music was seldom played publicly before the late 18th century). Orchestral, Opera, Gospel, Jazz and Rock'n'Roll and Rhythm and Blues (R&B) followed throughout the 1900s; each making a mark in their own right and earning the city merit as one of the most musically diverse in the country.

Fun Fact: Philadelphia's nickname, The City of Brotherly Love, is actually from the literal translation of its name in Greek as *Philos* means "love" and *Adelphos* means "brother."

When Dick Clark and American Bandstand (originally hosted by Bob Horn) began broadcasting, popular music was transformed and Philadelphia's local talent began to be recognized on a grand scale. In the 1960s, Philadelphia even produced an answer to Motown when the music dubbed "Philly Soul" began to take hold.

This long-running musical heritage produced many successful acts over the years and the 1980s were no different as rock'n'roll artists began finding varying degrees of achievement locally, nationally and internationally. The many success stories from that decade include Hall & Oates (actually originating in the mid 70s — their sound dubbed "blue-eyed soul" in keeping with their R&B roots), The Hooters, The A's, Tommy Conwell and Cinderella among others.

The stories that follow are just a few of my experiences with some of these and other homegrown acts… and one transplanted but locally notable DJ.

Smash Palace

Fall 1986

He who sings scares away his woes
— Cervantes

Philadelphia's Trocadero Theater, or the Troc as it's affectionately known, is a relatively small but popular rock club that frequently hosts local bands on the rise. One such band in the 80s was Smash Palace. Having been signed to Epic Records in 1985 and with their self-titled debut album quickly becoming a local favorite, they eventually earned some MTV airplay with the single *Living on the Borderline*. Introduced to their music by Kevin, I became an immediate fan and, as such, made sure to catch them live whenever possible.

Fun Fact: The Trocadero Theater was built in 1870 and opened as The Arch Street Opera House. Remodeled and renamed several times since, it was finally made into a concert hall and dance club in 1986. More than one-hundred years after opening, in June 1978, it was added to the National Register of Historic Places.

―――

With 'Til Tuesday at the Tower Theater in Upper Darby, PA and with The Outfield at Philadelphia's Chestnut Cabaret, I saw Smash Palace twice as an opening act. But the one time I saw them as headliners was at the Troc with Kevin in the fall of 1986. Parking a few blocks away on that cold night we walked briskly through the damp streets in eager anticipation of the night's show. Nearing the Arch Street entrance Kevin, perhaps in a subconsciously impulsive display of this anticipation, uncharacteristically began singing aloud the chorus to their song *Night of 1000 Faces*. At that time we both happened to look up and notice Smash Palace founder-guitarist-vocalist Steven Butler standing on the street outside the club. We were amused at the notion that this sudden vocal outburst may have appeared to be a veiled attempt to get his attention (it wasn't). In fact, in an unusual twist we didn't even make an effort to stop and introduce ourselves as would have been our more typical move. Our surprise at seeing him quickly passed and we continued on our way undeterred.

―――

Fun Fact: Though considered a Philadelphia band, Smash Palace was actually formed by brothers Steven and Brian Butler in Medford, NJ — the same small hometown where Kevin and I grew up. They remained residents of Medford during their initial and subsequent success and years later, during a reincarnation of the band, Kevin would have an opportunity to discuss music with Steven in his home.

As seating was general admission at the Troc, as you would expect we soon found ourselves migrating toward the front. By the time the band was in full swing we were front row at the chest-high stage. At some point during the show drummer Harry Lewis broke a stick. Flying forward it landed at the front of the stage and well within my reach. Naturally I leaned forward and grabbed it garnering yet another addition for my collection. Surprisingly large; the biggest one to this day, it's unusually flat-headed and wood-tipped, mostly unadorned with only a simple dark blue branding of name and band: *Harry L - Smash Palace.*

Fun Fact: In a "small world" moment… after becoming aware of Smash Palace I found an old 45-rpm record of a band called Skip 5 in a box in my sister Carole's basement. I noticed the drummer was the same Harry Lewis from Smash Palace, so I asked her where she got it. She said that she was "a friend of the drummer" and that they had worked together in an office some years before.

Soon after the show ended the band members blended in among the crowd, talking with friends and fans alike. At one point Harry came by and we began discussing the show, the band and drums. I asked what the highlight has been for him since having been signed to Epic and he replied that it was being awarded the opening slot for Australian rockers INXS during a Canadian tour. That reminded me of a comment he made nearly a year earlier when I met him in the lobby of the Tower Theater following their opening set for 'Til Tuesday. Asking how he felt about being signed to a major label, he responded that it was great but that he and the other band members still found themselves looking forward to "the next bigger thing."

Given that Smash Palace never attained the widespread

attention they would have liked (and that Kevin and I felt was deserved); perhaps that INXS gig would have to suffice.

Robert Hazard

December 1, 1986

*Once you make a decision,
the universe conspires to make it happen
— Ralph Waldo Emerson*

Songwriters are oftentimes; pardon the pun, the unsung heroes behind artists we all come to know and appreciate. Toiling away in relative anonymity, it's their hope that a performer will take at least one of their musical creations out into the world and find success with it — ideally at the top of the charts. There are also many singer-songwriters who, to varying degrees of success, do all these things themselves. Regardless of the method, a successful marriage between song and artist is often the result of one of two scenarios — either happenstance or patience and good decisions.

For Philadelphia singer-songwriter Robert Hazard the latter proved every bit the right approach when, after eight years of holding onto a song he referred to as a "gambler's diamond" he had tucked away for just the right time, he finally acquiesced and set it free. On the recommendation of his friend and producer Rick Chertoff (The Hooters, Joan Osborne, Sophie B. Hawkins), he agreed to let an unknown singer from New York record his prized possession. And so it was that in 1983 *Girls Just Wanna Have Fun*, sung by Queens native Cyndi Lauper, entered our collective consciousness reaching the number one spot on the charts in more than ten countries.

In 1986, as a student of Journalism at Burlington County College in New Jersey, I began writing for the school newspaper, The Word. Always in search of ways to tie my coursework, extra-curricular activities and newspaper articles to my interest in music, I somehow managed to secure an interview with Robert. As both a fan and fellow musician who covered his music in the earliest days of Upper Level, I was quite eager to do this interview — especially in his home. Though the resulting article, without apology, was clearly that of a novice; it was an enjoyable early effort for this aspirant writer and follows below in its entirety.

Sadly, on August 5, 2008, Robert succumbed to complications following surgery for pancreatic cancer. He was the third musician I met to have passed away and was only sixteen days shy of his sixtieth birthday.

Local Musician Has Risen to the Top of the Rock World

Just what is "a rock'n'roll event waiting to happen?" Well, according to Rolling Stone magazine it's Philadelphia's own Robert Hazard. And with the recent release of his third album, he took time to talk — despite just settling into his new Vincentown (NJ) home — about his start in the music business, his number-one single and the new album *Darling*.

As with most bands, Hazard started out playing local clubs and getting to know a little about the business along the way. It was during that time — 1978 to 1981 — that Robert Hazard and The Heroes developed a strong following of fans. So strong in fact, that when Hazard released the self-produced *Escalator of Life* EP in 1982, an album he described as "immediately gratifying," it sold more than 50,000 copies in the Philadelphia area.

These sales, along with increased airplay of the title track, resulted in RCA Records offering the group a contract. *Escalator'* was added to playlists across the country and a national tour was underway showing strong support in the Midwest and Los Angeles areas. "I had a strong relationship with KROQ in L.A.," said Hazard, who recently moved from Medford (NJ). "I got a lot of airplay out there."

In 1983 Hazard released his RCA debut album *Wing of Fire* which he said contains his best lyrical work. He became more visible to the public via TV appearances on Solid Gold and Bandstand and also played to an enthusiastic crowd of almost one million people on a 4th of July bill with the Beach Boys.

Then Hazard suddenly disappeared from the local scene. But that's not to say he wasn't busy. Between 1984 and 1986 he was working on new material for a follow up to *Wing of Fire* and working with Cyndi Lauper on her number-one single *Girls Just Wanna Have Fun.* "I actually wrote that song about seven or eight years ago in the bathtub," said Hazard.

Hazard's friend, who produced Lauper's *She's So Unusual* album, had always liked the song. So when he met with Lauper in New York he contacted Hazard and told him he found a girl to sing it.

Hazard met with Lauper for about a week and they worked on the song together. After its release it skyrocketed to number one and was on virtually every rock station in the world. It was picked as ASCAP's 1984 Top Pop Song of the Year. "She did it great," said Hazard. "At first it felt really weird because I wasn't recognized for it, but then the money and recognition started to come in and it felt good."

This November Hazard returned to the spotlight with the release of *Darling.* "I'm really happy with the new album," he said. "It's straightforward rock'n'roll."

One song on the album titled *Hip Pocket* was done in California with Rod Stewart's band. "We thought it would be a good idea because those guys are great," said Hazard. "It was a good experiment."

Hazard maintains that a single band in the studio isn't as good as having many musicians collaborating on a project. Though he writes almost all of the music and lyrics, he believes input from different musicians adds quality to the music. "When I go to the studio I call anyone I want," he said. However, on the road he does have a set band including Lou Franco and Roger Girk on guitars, Joe McGinty on bass, Bill Robinson on keyboards and Tommy Gettes on drums.

You can catch Hazard at the Ambler Cabaret in Ambler on December 6, at Reading's Silo on December 7, at the Barn in Bensalem on December 26 and New Year's Eve at the Garden State Race Track.

When asked if he had any advice for aspiring musicians he said, "Stay in your room and write songs — that is the key to everything."

Hazard believes that in order to be successful you have to give the people what they want. He should know. He's been doing just that for ten years.

The Hooters

Fall 1989

The mode by which the inevitable comes to pass is effort
— Oliver Wendell Holmes

Although I had seen The Hooters in 1983 for the first time, it wasn't until a few years later when Kevin more extensively introduced me to their music that I came to further appreciate them. And as we had seen them live several times since, often during the earliest days of Upper Level, their influence both on our writing and approach became somewhat evident; a sort of unofficial template for what we hoped to accomplish.

Though we didn't emulate the specifics of their early reggae-ska-rock sound or make use of their unconventional namesake melodica (the hooter), we did approach our overall sound with them serving at least somewhat as an inspiration. And we may have borrowed a bit from their look as well — although admittedly I was the most blatant in this regard having adopted the sartorial canary-yellow accents of drummer Dave Uosikkinen. But the rest of the guys in Upper Level, perhaps to their credit, were less inclined to be so calculated. As for The Hooters' music; we covered much of it early on even recording a handful of those songs in a makeshift studio in Chris's parent's basement. It was a time of determined musical navigation, the upshot of which was the most steady and creative original band any of us were ever in.

Kevin and I had seen The Hooters play more than a dozen times — as an opening act, a headliner and even as part of assorted ensemble offerings in celebration of various milestone birthdays for reigning local rock station WMMR. Whether in small local clubs like the Chestnut Cabaret, mid-size venues such as the 5000-seat, eighty-year-old Tower Theater or the 18,000-seat Spectrum; we've seen them in all phases of their rise to musical prominence. And prior to reconnecting with one another in 1985, Kevin and I each saw them at our respective alma maters — Temple University and Glassboro State College — before they signed with Columbia Records. But perhaps the biggest stage we ever saw them on, both literally and figuratively, was at JFK Stadium in Philadelphia on July 13, 1985 when they opened the United States portion of Live Aid.

But it was in the smaller Cabaret settings where the best shows seemed to happen and where better interactive opportunities arose. During a record-release party at the former 23 East Cabaret in Ardmore, PA I managed a sort of fragmented meet-and-greet outside before the show. Though going about my usual activities where bands and shows were concerned, I decided on a different approach this time. Rather than join the crowds that would typically gather to meet them *after* a show, I decided to wait outside the backstage door and catch them on their way *in*.

Fun Fact: Earlier that year as Kevin, my friend Dennis (who, in 1987 in response to his energetic audience participation, was invited onto the Spectrum stage by John Mellencamp to sing the closing chorus on *Pink Houses*) and I were passing through Center City Philadelphia heading to a Hooters show at the Tower Theater, we spotted their singer-guitarist Eric Bazilian on Market Street. So we had Dennis stop the car in the middle of the street so we could hop out and say hello. As he circled the block Kevin and I introduced ourselves to Eric, who was very cordial and quite agreeable to having his picture taken with us. When Dennis made his way back around we hopped in the car and two hours later were watching Eric and the Hooters onstage playing to a typically sold-out hometown crowd.

It was after dark and the back lot was dimly lit and quiet, only a faint sound bleeding through from the club. Seeing no signs of life in any direction — and as it was getting close to show time — I began to wonder if the band had already entered through the front door. Just then a white Jeep Cherokee pulled up and stopped.

From The Inside

The passenger door opened and a dim light shone on keyboardist Rob Hyman as he said a quick goodbye to his wife and stepped out. Keeping a socially respectful distance I offered some sort of casual greeting and he replied in kind, asking if I was going in to see the show. Saying I was, he wished me "a good time" and quickly disappeared inside.

Resembling Eric at the time; somewhat facially and with my long, dark hair and similar height and build, I was amused by the brief but humorous case of mistaken identity that occurred next.

Shortly after Rob made his way inside, a small group of people heading toward me appeared in the distance. Though only visible in silhouette; the streetlamp from behind casting their shadows in my direction, as they neared I was relieved to hear the gist of their exchange as casual, upbeat and peppered with moments of laughter. Once within earshot, all of us still mostly shrouded in darkness, one of them unexpectedly called out, "Hey Eric — what's up? What are you doing out here?" I immediately announced that I wasn't Eric just as they grew close enough to see. It was then that I realized it was two more band members, bassist Fran Smith, Jr. and guitarist John Lilley, with some friends. As they saw me more clearly they expressed amusement at the misled resemblance. We exchanged casual but brief introductions; shaking hands then parting ways as they entered the club and I walked to the front to join the growing crowd awaiting the start of the show.

After the set, which showcased their new album *Zig Zag* in its entirety (exciting in the intimate confines of the 23 East), I hung around to see what else might await me. A few handshakes and introductions were great, but I sometimes viewed these as potential opportunities to take things to the next level. It wasn't dissatisfaction with the experience, but more an effort just to see where I could take it (and preferably to get a drumstick). So as the crowd thinned and I saw the drum technician (or drum tech) dismantling Dave's kit, I approached asking if he had any spare sticks he might be willing to part with. He reached over to the floor tom and picked up a pair that Dave set down after the last song and handed them to me without saying much. Although cordial, his willingness to quickly help seemed more an effort to get rid of me than to satisfy my personal want of a souvenir. Regardless, I thanked him kindly and walked away.

Having an endorsement deal with Pro-Mark at this time, Dave's nylon-tipped sticks were stamped with both his signature and the band name as it appears on the *One Way Home* album: *Pro-Mark - USA - Hickory - David Uosikkinen - Hooters.* Nearly twenty years later I still have those sticks, Dave is still recording and touring with The Hooters and Kevin and I continue to see them whenever possible; most recently at The Electric Factory in Philadelphia on November 21, 2007 when they performed with the reunited and legendary 80s Philadelphia band The A's.

WMMR: Pierre Robert Interview

February 1, 1990

The dimensions of the radio are truly to be treasured
— Charles Osgood

In 1990, during the final months of working toward my undergraduate degree in Communications / Journalism at Glassboro State College (now Rowan University) in New Jersey, I was again writing for the school newspaper; this time The Whit. As with all previous efforts at tying my coursework to music whenever possible, I managed an interview with the popular and well-respected Philadelphia radio DJ, Pierre Robert.

As a listener of Pierre's since high school, when he came to Philadelphia's WMMR from San Francisco's KSAN, I was quite eager to interview him — especially as the invitation included doing so in the studio prior to his afternoon airtime shift (with a further offer to remain for the show). The resulting article, which follows and is somewhat improved from my previous interview efforts, is just another early attempt to peek behind the musical curtain and gain perspective on yet another side of the "business" of music.

In the nearly thirty years since his arrival, Pierre has become somewhat of an icon in Philadelphia; equal parts well-respected DJ, ambassador of good will (and good music and good karma) and an overall and firmly transplanted "personality extraordinaire." As such, he seems well-poised to continue his affair with the City of Brotherly Love as long as the "good citizens" of Philadelphia (as he has long referred to his faithful listeners) continue to reciprocate.

Pierre Robert Spins Midday Melodies for the Masses

In the world of competitive radio there are morning-show rock jocks and then there are midday-shift disc jockeys (DJs) who must follow these morning shows. WMMR's Pierre Robert (pronounced Ro-Bear) is one such DJ and is considered the "reigning king" of the midday shift (10:00AM — 2:00PM). As such, he has no reservations about this time slot on the air. "I like following the Morning Zoo," said Robert. "It's a great job."

Resembling a rock'n'roller with his elbow-length hair, mustache and beard and faded jeans, Robert began his radio career in his hometown of San Francisco about eleven years ago. Unsure of what he wanted to do with his life after high school, he enrolled in broadcasting school just outside of San Francisco. While there, he spent a year learning about the inner workings of the world of radio broadcasting and soon after became a volunteer for 95 KSAN-FM in San Francisco.

While working at KSAN, Robert got his big break to go on the air before he was even hired as a DJ. "One night someone wasn't there for his shift, so I told my boss that I thought I could do it," he said. "So he said to me, 'Kid, you're on.'"

Robert was then hired to continue as a DJ

at KSAN, a job he kept for about two years. When the ratings started to drop, the station turned from a rock'n'roll format to country music. About six months later he left.

With no formal plan and no job, Robert and a friend decided to head east. They traveled across country in Robert's Volkswagen van, or as he affectionately refers to it, "Minerva." Unfortunately Minerva didn't last long in Philadelphia. "She's no more," he lamented. "She was my friend, but she got towed away to a junkyard and I didn't get her out in time."

Minerva was towed away due to Robert's penchant for not paying parking tickets - $1,006 worth to be exact. His on-air pleas to listeners to help him find Minerva proved successful when a man called in and said that he had located her in a local junkyard. By the time Robert reached the junkyard, however, Minerva was little more than scrap metal. "At least I saved myself from paying $1,006," he said. "But I don't think it was worth it."

In 1980, despite losing Minerva, things began to look up for Robert in the area of radio. Starting as a music librarian full time and working part time on weekends as a DJ, he soon became one of the regular on-air personalities at 93.3 WMMR in 1981. For almost one and a half years, Robert handled the overnight shift (2am — 6am), five days a week. He eventually worked his way into the midday slot which is where he remains today.

Reflecting on his decision to get into radio broadcasting, the 5-foot, 9-inch tall vegetarian said he's glad he did it. "It's definitely the best job I ever had and it's a great gig for the moment," he said.

Consistently retaining the largest daytime audiences in the Philadelphia radio market, Robert, relaxing on a sofa in the small but comfortable studio lounge, also realizes the potential downside of success. "It feels great to be number one, or at least in the top three. However, it's humbling because this is a very fickle business," he said emphatically. "I respect it, but it's fleeting."

Following the Morning Zoo, Philadelphia's top-rated morning show, isn't exactly easy according to Robert, but he has his own philosophy on why the audience stays tuned in. "John DeBella (morning DJ) is like a cup of coffee; he gets everyone up in the morning," said Robert. "I'm more like a cup of herbal tea, I keep them up."

Robert believes that people's energy levels build as the day progresses, but not if they're always on full steam. He sees his job as one that keeps the listeners going without tiring them out, as a steady diet of the Zoo might do. "Most listeners are in work all day and they don't want to have to concentrate on the radio the whole time," he said.

Every week there is a music meeting between Program Director Ted Utz, DJ and Assistant Program Director Joe Bonadonna and Music Director Erin Riley. This committee of three must decide which of the albums received weekly, if any, will get airplay. "Every week we receive about five or so albums from knowns and unknowns," said Robert. "We try to balance the old with the new."

According to Robert there is a lot more to being a DJ than most people think. "It's not so much a physical job as it is a mental one," he said. "You always have to be ahead of the game."

Besides his on-air responsibilities of spinning records, running commercials and taking record requests, Robert also has many outside obligations. "I do club appearances one or two nights a week and often three or four nights," he said. "Mostly it's fun and it's voluntary."

He contends that a part of WMMR's success is attributed to the fact that it is always doing something which involves the listeners directly. "We're successful because we're out in the public; people get to see a face behind a voice," he said. Some notable events that Robert has hosted with WMMR are the station's 20th birthday party held at the Spectrum, the annual "DeBella DeBall" and the annual "Louie Louie" parade as well.

Although he is compensated for his work outside the station, he will do free benefits if he believes in the cause. Some of his outside work includes attending concerts; this is the "easiest and definitely the most fun" of all his jobs as a DJ, he said.

During his time with WMMR he has interviewed the likes of David Lee Roth, Pat Benatar, Bob Geldof, The Beach Boys, Van Halen and Jack Nicholson. But his favorite interview was with a member of his favorite band, Crosby, Stills and Nash. "Graham Nash was here and he even sang a song over the radio," said Robert.

He also recalled his most memorable interview. "It was Justin Hayward of the Moody Blues; he said that I was his favorite interview," he said fondly.

Although he has benefited from his job in different ways, Robert said he's hoping to improve people's daily lives through his show. "I'd like to be considered someone who can make a positive difference in some way," he said. "I like to make people feel better by playing songs — that's what I'm all about."

FOURTEEN
John Mellencamp: Backstage Moments

January 15, 1992

Where there is an open mind there will always be a frontier
— Charles Kettering

For the most part my efforts at getting backstage, meeting bands, collecting drumsticks and so forth were by design a solo effort when not done with Kevin. And I never minded going it alone as the sense of exploration was always appealing and easily half of what made it successful; nobody to slow me down or otherwise impede my progress. But the one person I *did* make an exception for was Kelley.

We had gone to a few concerts together while dating. The first one — only two weeks into our relationship — was Polish-born singer-songwriter Basia at the Tower Theater on August 10, 1990. Though I had discovered her music during college, I never saw her live prior to that show. During the next year and half Kell and I saw a number of other concerts — to include Hall & Oates, Aerosmith, Kenny G and Billy Joel among others — but I never attempted to get backstage at any of them as it simply didn't cross my mind, certainly not to the extent that I pursued it. But when we went to our first John Mellencamp show together I decided I'd give it a shot.

Though my appreciation for his music was fairly complete and long-predated my time with Kell, she was mostly familiar with whatever hits he had at the time. After warming up to much of his catalog soon after that show however, she quickly counted him among her favorite artists.

Following the two-hour performance in support of his eleventh album *Whenever We Wanted,* I paid a visit to my old friend and Spectrum security guard Larry Jasper. Though we only connected when I attended concerts, he always had a warm smile for me — albeit occasionally preceded by a mocking roll of the eyes and turn of the head as if to say, "Oh no… not *again!"* But he truly did become somewhat of a friend within the context of these shows and as evident by our discussions throughout the years he seemed to enjoy our intermittent showtime get-togethers.

It was probably a bit of a surprise for Larry to see me approach with someone in tow. But I wanted to introduce Kell to him… and get us backstage as Kell was even *more* eager to meet John than I was. Soon after introducing them and making some small talk I broached the backstage topic with Larry and found him to be unusually quickly receptive to the idea. Although he was always quite amiable and had no problem letting me back whenever he could, it was typically after some careful consideration about what band it was, who might be watching him and so on. This time however, perhaps in deference to Kell, he allowed us to pass — seemingly without a second thought. Regardless why, I gladly accepted, thanked him and headed back to the meet-and-greet room with which I had become somewhat familiar during the past seven years.

Soon Kell and I were mixing with the band; chatting and taking pictures with each of them and wondering if John was going to show (he didn't). My personal highlight was meeting and taking a picture with John's long-time studio and touring drummer at the time, the phenomenal Kenny Aronoff. Kell was happy to pose (always with her engaging smile) for a picture with guitarist Mike Wanchic and the both of us somehow ended up in a shot with bassist

Toby Myers and his Aunt Molly. He introduced her to us before we took the shot and it became somewhat of a running joke with us afterwards; "… and here's a picture of us with bassist Toby and Aunt Molly."

Fun Fact: As our time backstage was ending I asked "Aunt Molly" if she planned to keep the round, orange stick-on pass she had on her jacket (immediately recognizing it as a unique keepsake of the night and assuming she saw no value in it aside from its intended purpose). I was happy to hear her say I could have it and she graciously handed it to me on the spot as I thanked her. As evident by the picture at the beginning of this chapter, it's still pressed beneath the clear laminate in a photo album with pictures from both the show and our time backstage; one of which shows Aunt Molly still wearing the pass which reads: *John Mellencamp / Whenever We Wanted / After Show Only.*

All in all it was another great concert and not a bad ending to a night out with my then-girlfriend Kell. I asked her to marry me nine days later. I don't think my ability to get us backstage had anything to do with her accepting my proposal… at least I don't *think* it did. Hmm…

FIFTEEN
A Van Halen Soundcheck

April 28, 1995

I get by with a little help from my friends
— *John Lennon*

Although I had seen Van Halen in concert on every tour from 1979 through 1984 inclusive, more than a decade had passed since that last show. And when David Lee Roth left the band the following year, replaced by Sammy Hagar, two groups of fans quickly emerged each taking a hard line on either side of the musically-political fence. Though undeniably in the Dave camp, when they came to town with Sammy in 1995, I found good reason to make my way to the Spectrum — though not so much for the actual show.

After seventeen years of attending concerts there, to include some pretty good extra-curricular activities both during and after shows, I finally had an in for a potential pre-show moment and I wanted to seize it. That said, and any party affiliations aside, I began to set the wheels in motion to make it happen.

The "in" I had was my good friend Paul, at the time a chef at the Spectrum's Ovations Club restaurant. Part of our long friendship included sharing a fondness for some bands, not the least of which was Van Halen. And just as he, Dan and I experienced our first concert together in 1978 (Boston), so, too, did we attend all those early Van Halen shows together, though oftentimes joined by others. So when it was announced that they were touring again — with a stop in Philadelphia — I asked Paul if he'd be able to help get me into the arena early. He simply and willingly suggested I pay him a visit on the afternoon of the show at which time he'd get me into Ovations. Once in, as always, I'd have to figure it out as I went along.

Fun Fact: After twenty-two years apart Van Halen reunited with David Lee Roth in 2007 for what would become one of their most successful tours. Although original bassist Michael Anthony was not involved; replaced by Eddie Van Halen's son Wolfgang, the focus was clearly on the coming together of Dave and Eddie as they had been at the center of the 1985 split. In keeping with our personal history — as well as the night's reunion theme — Paul, Dan and I attended the October 1, 2007 show at Philadelphia's Wachovia Center (which during the course of this writing was once again renamed — this time as the Wells Fargo Center), with Dan having flown in from Ohio specifically for this show. Added to the old threesome, of course, was Kevin who actually knew Paul and Dan quite well. Even Brad Scott was there, at the time General Manager of the venue's Victor Club restaurant (more about his connection later). He and Paul arranged for complimentary food and drinks for us beforehand at the Victor Club and during the show in our private Club Box seats. What a difference a couple of decades (and a couple of contacts) can make when going to a concert.

Informing Kevin that I had yet another adventure planned, I asked if he wanted to join me and without hesitation he said he was in. I arrived at the arena on show day and pulled into a parking lot adjacent to the backstage loading ramp where, in our younger years, friends and I often hung around before and after concerts hoping to catch a glimpse of the bands coming or going. I told the parking attendant of my "appointment" with the chef at Ovations and she ushered me through the gate. Things were looking up.

When I mentioned my meeting to the guard at the bottom of the ramp, he said I was expected and picked up the phone. A moment later in full chef gear — sans toque — Paul came strolling out and walked me in. After some small talk, a quick tour of Ovations and an escort to the seating area, Paul headed back to work leaving me to do whatever it was I was going to do. Though in parting — and perhaps in a moment of apprehension at assisting in my activities — he also included some not-so-subtle advice to lay low in the process (translation: don't get him fired).

Soon after he left I made my way back to the loading ramp to see if Kevin had arrived — he had. Advising the guard that he was with me, we headed inside and made our way back to the house, choosing first-level seats with a diagonal view from stage right. I'm not sure why we didn't opt for floor seating as that would seem the logical choice given that we had full run of the place. Regardless, our view was excellent and we were practically the only ones there.

After a brief wait, all efforts at arranging this opportunity paid off when Van Halen took the stage, albeit without Sammy, and began preparing for the soundcheck. A few rows behind us were a group of guys that Van Halen bassist Michael Anthony began joking with from his spot onstage. We soon discovered they were members of the opening act, Georgia alternative band Collective Soul.

Drummer Alex Van Halen stepped behind his most recent and always extravagant Ludwig drum kit as younger brother and guitarist Eddie, suffering from hip issues at the time, took his place onstage with the use of a cane while periodically resting on a stool at his microphone. After a few minutes of tweaking knobs, tapping drums and speaking to the front of house (or FOH) sound guys, they launched into *When It's Love* from their 1988 album *OU812*. It was both exciting and interesting to hear it played essentially as an instrumental with only Michael and Eddie singing backing vocals for the first line of each chorus. Moments like that made these excursions all the more unique and appealing — especially from this musician's perspective.

At one point during the song Paul came out and took a seat with us to catch some of their performance. Although he didn't stay long, I was glad to see my friend and fellow Van Halen fan taking advantage of this perk of his job — especially given that he's the one who made it possible for Kevin and me. Though it was a relatively brief, one-song soundcheck, it was well worth the time, effort and drive into the city.

Fun Fact: The only time I saw Van Halen post-Roth was on August 6, 1986 during their *5150* tour. I went with Kevin and after the show we decided to drive to the Four Seasons Hotel figuring if they were staying there we might be able to meet them. Soon after we arrived, a limo pulled up and out stepped Eddie. As we and a few other fans began to approach, a bodyguard spread his arms blocking us from making any contact. But Eddie, to his credit, gently brushed him aside and reached out to shake our hands.

When the soundcheck was over, Kevin and I made our way down to the floor behind the stage where we happened upon Michael (Alex and Eddie having somehow already disappeared). As we each shook his hand and introduced ourselves, I handed my camera to the nearest person who quickly took a shot of us all standing together. I then asked where the other guys were and, gesturing toward the backstage area, he replied, "Probably back there somewhere." We then thanked him and went our separate ways — he likely heading "back there somewhere" and Kevin and I returning to Ovations.

After detailing our encounter to Paul and taking a seat at the bar, we discussed whether to stay for the show — which was still more than a few hours off. But as we were talking I grew increasingly restive, not content to just sit there knowing that Eddie, Alex and Sammy were somewhere in the building. So I decided to see if I could find them while Kevin, ever cautious, decided to stay behind and thereby eliminate any risk of being ejected.

My search was essentially limited to the inner corridor; the business area beneath the seats which runs the entire circumference of the Spectrum and where all offices, locker rooms and media rooms are located. Passing several offices and open doors along the way, including Flyers and 76ers offices, I saw nothing of note. That is, until I came to one door with an entrance hall leading to a room at the far end. I stopped and looked in — fewer than twenty feet away on a sofa with his guitar on a stand next to him sat Eddie Van Halen. I knew this was what I came for, but suddenly felt slightly unsettled by the notion of being so intrusive. I paused to consider the potential consequences of just walking in. Then quickly realizing I had nothing to lose, I slowly — respectfully — entered.

In an effort to casually catch his attention, I offered a deliberately low-key, "Excuse me," as I approached. When he looked up I continued somewhat subdued both to lessen my imposition and to put him at ease. By the time I said I was with Ovations and there to say a quick "hello" before leaving for the day, I was fully in the room with a handful of people all around.

Immediately to my left was Sammy putting a mixture of fruit into a blender and making some type of health drink while on my right stood a few guys from the band's entourage. Eddie was still sitting on the sofa directly in front of me when one of the guys stepped up, asked who I was and what I was doing there. I repeated my vague Ovations story stressing that I was simply hoping to get a quick picture with Eddie and Sammy if they wouldn't mind. And just as he began shaking his head and telling me to leave, Sammy interrupted, "Sure, I'll take a picture with you."

Clearly not happy with Sammy's generosity the guy said to me, "Okay, you want a picture? Here you go," as he held the camera at arm's length and took a picture of himself giving the finger. Then Sammy said, "Come on, give the guy a break and just take a picture for him," as he walked toward me and put his arm around my shoulder. The guy finally went along with it and took the shot as Sammy urged Eddie to get up and pose as well — which he did. I then shook hands with both of them, thanked them and left.

Instead of heading to my car I made my way back to Ovations

where I found Kevin still sitting at the end of the bar, presumably waiting for me to return with a story of success or failure. Walking toward him and holding up my camera as if in some victory march, I announced that he should have come with me. Anticipating my story, Paul saw me return and quickly joined us as I began sharing the details.

But only moments into my recap a couple of guys, who I later assumed must have been band security staff, entered the restaurant asking if I was there. Brad Scott, Ovations General Manager at the time, brought them over to the end of the bar and they began asking me to remove the film from my camera (this was before the advent of digital cameras and well before cell phone cameras). I immediately declined, asking why they wanted it. But they pressed on repeatedly and without explanation, "Give us the film… just give us the film." I deferred to Kevin, an attorney, who began by asking the same question I did about their reason for wanting it. But I interrupted, defending what I assumed to be my right to have taken the pictures by stressing that "Sammy and Eddie *said* I could take them — they even *posed* with me!"

"Give us the film," was their only response. Finally, primarily in deference to Paul and Brad — and also in an effort to keep this still relatively inconspicuous matter from getting any further out of control — I acquiesced and began to open my camera exposing the film. But before I could even take it out, one of the guys reached in, pulled it out and handed the camera back to me. Both of them then turned and left without any further question or comment.

To this day it remains one of the strangest and most tense backstage moments I've experienced — and an unfortunate end to an otherwise successful, albeit unauthorized, meet-and-greet.

Part II:
BELONGING THERE

He was a simple man
Never needed much more than
A song in his heart

UNTAMED HEARTS / 1994

•••••••••••••••••••••••

SIXTEEN
A Return to Rush

August 4, 2004

You are the music while the music lasts
— T.S. Eliot

Canadian band Rush had an early influence on me soon after discovering them during my freshman year of high school. And my appreciation only grew after seeing them in concert for the first time on September 25, 1980. During the ensuing five years, after countless album spins and a few more live shows, I came to respect their musicianship; particularly the talents of drummer-lyricist Neil Peart. As a fellow drummer with a tendency for a more disciplined approach, I easily related to his playing style; thoroughly enjoyable yet taxing enough to continually challenge my abilities — even to this day. And the stories woven by his thought-provoking, sometimes reflective lyrics coupled with my interest in the written word further sustained that admiration. Thirty years later, despite an eighteen-year period of relative apathy toward their newer music, I maintain a high regard for both the band and the man.

On a hot and sunny August 4, 2004, the day of my first Rush concert since 1986, I decided to head early to the Tweeter Center in Camden, NJ to take in whatever early activities may be occurring and to see if I'd be able to get inside for a close-up look at the pre-show world of live music. After only a few minutes ambling around the parking lot I ended up casually entering the arena via an unlocked door. Although there was an older gentleman sitting at what appeared to be a security desk behind a glass partition to my left, by a stroke of luck and good timing, he happened to be looking away as I sauntered by unnoticed.

Perhaps it was my professional shirt-and-tie look (complete with a work ID hanging around my neck) that kept anyone from asking who I was or why I was there and I soon realized I was walking around unopposed. I was inside seemingly without any concerns and, as such, free to make my way to the house for a look at the stage.

I discovered the entrance area to be a much different place when not crowded with all the usual suspects; fans going every which way, food-and-drink vendors tending to the masses and merchandisers hawking t-shirts, tour books and other assorted band memorabilia. Far more spacious and infinitely quieter, it's almost like a temporary sanctuary of the concert hall. But all of that would change dramatically only a few hours later when, as the venue staff stated, it was "doors open."

Finding my way to the house I was soon viewing all the onstage gear to include — most impressively to me — Neil's drums. They absolutely captivated me and from a distance, actually the front row, with my camera in hand I asked Neil's drum tech, Lorne Wheaton, if he wouldn't mind taking a picture from behind the kit for me. Much to my surprise he benignly replied, "You can come up here and take a few for yourself if you want."

I hesitated at first giving a moment of thought to the possibility that I may have misheard him. But I soon found myself onstage amid Alex's guitars, Geddy's basses and Neil's custom-made DW kit (specially designed for the *R30* tour and dubbed the S.S. Professor) — primarily Black with Sparkle inlays around images representing five Rush albums. While taking note of the striking gold-plated hardware and the bright finish of the Sabian cymbals, I made some small talk with Lorne as he continued tending to the business at hand. But despite his kind invitation I began to feel a bit intrusive. So, not wanting to overstay my welcome, I quickly snapped those few shots of the kit, thanked him for the opportunity and returned to the seats.

As I preferred not being at the show in my work clothes (especially in the 90-degree heat), I decided to forgo the 5:00PM soundcheck (what was I thinking?) and head home to change into something a bit more concert friendly.

Fun Fact: In December 2006, more than two years after this concert and after reading Neil's third book, *Traveling Music*, I was motivated to write a letter to him commenting not only on the book but also on the *R30* show and how both inspired me to revisit my lifelong passion for drumming as I had been relatively indifferent toward it during those years when life was taking over. I also wanted to make him aware of how cordial and accommodating Lorne was to me:

December 19, 2006

Neil:

Despite having written hundreds of personal letters throughout my life I never quite knew how I would begin writing to someone I didn't know other than through his or her work, and as such never attempted it. Nevertheless here I am doing just that and discovering that expressing my apprehension is proving to be a fine opening — or at least a viable one.

Anyway, my intent is quite simply to thank you for being an indirect yet vital source of inspiration for the return of my musical activities — and for taking me on some vividly wonderful tours of the United States (and the world) in 1600 or so pages. If

I may elaborate just a bit...

Having spent the better part of my forty-one years admiring your music and your contributions to *Modern Drummer* and having more recently become an avid reader of your books, I always felt the archetypical connection between fan and artist (especially as a fellow drummer and lyricist). However, I rarely sensed a need to make any real connection with you or the band — at least not to the extent that I'd join a fan club, seek an autograph, or (gasp!) write a fan letter.

I was always of the belief that the reality wouldn't live up to the visualization. As you so aptly affirm in *Roadshow*, "I realized that sometimes it was better not to visit the places of your dreams — better to leave them as exotic, soft-focus mirages of romance." Exactly! Yet, somehow that notion changed for me before, during and after a show I attended on the *R30* tour in August 2004.

Sometime between 1996 and 2004 I lost track of my musical drive and involvement. I had written and recorded several songs up until late 1992 (including my wedding song), but no longer felt a bond with any music and essentially put down my sticks — and pen — for much of that time. It wasn't until late 2004, after reading *Ghost Rider*, that the following words you wrote resonated with me, albeit for drastically dissimilar reasons, "...but I'm not yet sure about art or music (I can look at it or listen to it, but not with the same "engagement" I used to)." Included in that retreat was a disconnect with any new Rush material and when my friend Kevin asked if I wanted to go to a show in 2002 I declined out of lack of interest (now quite fond of *Vapor Trails* I wish I had gone).

In 2004, having heard about the upcoming 30th Anniversary tour, I simply decided I'd like to see

Rush again. So I asked Kevin if he was interested (he was) and I purchased the tickets.

While at work on "a hot and *sunny* August afternoon," I decided I'd had enough for the day (one of the benefits — and potential pitfalls — of a sales profession). I was keyed up at the thought of that evening's show and instead of going home decided to head directly to the Camden, NJ venue to take in whatever pre-show activity might be occurring. After only a few minutes ambling around the parking lot with my ever-present camera I ended up casually entering the outdoor arena. Perhaps it was my professional shirt-and-tie look that kept anyone from asking who I was even though I quite openly and politely said hello to some staff once inside.

At first I sincerely felt concerned about trespassing and considered leaving almost immediately. Then, knowing I meant no harm and would respect certain boundaries (my existing infraction aside), my sense of guilt lifted and curiosity kicked in. Before long I realized I was practically the only one there (save the stage hands).

Seeing all the gear onstage from a distance — Alex's guitars and amps, Geddy's basses and pedals, and the pièce de résistance for me, your drums — your life *within* the cymbals — absolutely captivated me. So I sat quietly in the front row taking in the onstage bustle. Soon Lorne came out to do his "drum teching" and I simply continued to watch. Eventually, holding up my camera, I summoned the will to ask if he wouldn't mind taking a shot from behind the kit for me. To my utter astonishment he benignly replied, "You can come up here and take a few for yourself if you want." Wow.

I hesitated at first, feeling part of that connection I never wanted to make before, but soon found myself at the riser. Examining the kit I took note of the striking gold-plated hardware and bright finish of the cymbals while making some small talk with Lorne as he continued tending to the business at hand. Despite his kind invitation I felt a bit intrusive and didn't want to overstay my welcome. So after quickly snapping a few shots (including a close-up of the laminated "1st SET" set list affixed to the top of your bass drum), I thanked him and returned to my seat.

After giving some thought to hanging around for the soundcheck, I quickly abandoned that idea. Though I knew it would be thrilling to be an audience of one, I also thought the prospect of meeting you (or Alex or Geddy) under those conditions may not prove rewarding. Rather, I considered that any unsolicited advance would be invasive, uncomfortable and just plain wrong. Besides, I was already there illicitly no matter how inoffensively. So I left the venue and headed home only to return later that evening to see the show under more proper conditions of admission (for what it's worth, I provided a review of the August 4 show on the website).

This is where my thanks applies because it was immediately following the show that I felt a need to reacquaint myself with music. In that two-hour period I was ostensibly transported out of my recent indifference toward music to a place where drumming and writing seemed as inviting and potentially stimulating as when I picked up my first pair of sticks 28 years prior. My response to that instant exhilaration was equally swift and I jumped in with both feet — and hands as it were.

During the next several months I built a comfortable music room in my basement (a journal note from that time: "Can't wait to complete it so I can move my drums in!"). I relished the project of stripping and rewrapping in a gloss-black veneer my old, well-kept, metallic-white Tama Royalstars. I then shined up my cymbals and hardware and spent many wonderful months reconnecting with my musical side. *A Work In Progress* had its place in this endeavor while introducing me to *Test for Echo*. I now look forward to exploring soloing techniques when I order *Anatomy of a Drum Solo*.

As a result of the inspiration brought into being during the afternoon and evening of that *R30* show, drumming, writing new songs and reworking some old ones have once again become kinetically enjoyable pursuits. The active reintroduction of music into my life has been fulfilling and for lack of any other reason (not that I was searching for one) I can sincerely say it was a combination of Lorne's obliging invitation to those few moments at your kit and that evening's show that "brought it all home" for me. *The Masked Rider, Ghost Rider, Traveling Music* and *Roadshow* have all just been icing on the proverbial cake as I enjoyed them immensely and I now eagerly await your next offering.

As a final note, I feel the inception of my musical renovation and the concurrent readings of your books have one small study worthy of mention. Whereas I would typically favor following the order of release when reading a specific author, of your three books in print at the time I uncharacteristically chose to read *Traveling Music* first (largely based on the subtitle). I was enthused by this choice, and further found myself smiling, upon reading Nietzsche's quote at the outset: "Without music, life would be a mistake."

How timely. How fitting. Thanks again.

Musically,

Russ DiBella

PS: Three guys are discussing their respective IQs. The first guy says his is 145 and the others ask what he does for a living. He replies that he's a nuclear physicist. The second guy says that his IQ is 125. The others ask his occupation and he replies that he's a brain surgeon. The third guy says his IQ is 75 and the others turn to him and ask, "So, how long have you been a drummer?"

Ouch.

Nearly a year later, quite unexpectedly, I received a handwritten and signed postcard reply postmarked November 26, 2007:

"Hello Russ, Thank you for your nice letter, and I'm glad Lorne was so nice to you — he's good to me, too! All the best to you — Neil Peart."

In the interim I once again saw Rush on July 6, 2007 during the first leg of their *Snakes & Arrows* tour. Soon after, Neil posted a comment on his website indicating that he ordered one-hundred postcards to send as thank-you notes to all the fans who sent things to him on this tour. Although my letter clearly predates that time, I'm quite pleased to have the postcard as part of my memorabilia no matter the circumstances.

That was my first experience accessing the Tweeter pre-show under the guise of belonging there simply by way of a white shirt, tie and work ID. Who knew? My only regret was not asking Lorne for a drumstick. Unfortunately, with the excitement and shock at having gotten far as I did still palpable, it just never came to mind. Further, it was their milestone *R30* tour in celebration of their 30th anniversary and those special edition sticks would have been nice to have — especially for this longtime Neil Peart fan and "student." Oh well... lesson certainly learned.

As noted in the letter, the Rush website had an area where fans could post reviews from shows seen on this tour. And as I saw that as another opportunity to merge writing with music, upon arrival home that night I put pen to paper, so to speak, and posted a review while the details were still fresh in my mind (and the ringing still in my ears):

> At the risk of sounding erroneously blasé, Rush's performance at the Camden, NJ Tweeter Center was not surprising at all. It was — as it always has been both live and on record — an impressively brilliant display of musical finesse spanning three decades and representing thirteen of their eighteen studio releases (including their most recent cover effort *Feedback*).
>
> As the members, Alex Lifeson, Geddy Lee, and Neil Peart, whetted the audience's collective appetite by opening with a seamless instrumental medley of early works, I found myself intuitively covering for Lee's vocal absence while trying to anticipate where one song would blend into the next. Rolling directly into 1980's *The Spirit of Radio*, they continued their decade-jumping musical journey taking us from 1987 to 1993, from 1982 to 2002, etc.
>
> While many radio staples were present during the show by way of *Subdivisions, Tom Sawyer* and *Working Man*, many other favorites were plentiful and culled from the depths of *Hemispheres, Fly By Night, 2112* and *A Farewell to Kings* as well as more recent releases *Roll the Bones* and *Counterparts*.
>
> Requesting a pardon for their "bit of indulgence," Lee introduced the first of four *Feedback* cover tunes we'd be privy to that night as they launched into The Who's *The Seeker* before rounding out the first set with *One Little Victory* from 2002's *Vapor Trails*, bringing them up-to-date with

their most recent original release.

One fifteen-minute interlude later found us witnessing their comedic side via an animated short entitled *That Darn Dragon* in which the band members find themselves battling a troublemaking dragon. Following this they again took the stage and continued to roll out the 30th Anniversary retrospective in fine form displaying their respective instrumental prowess on the riff and fill-heavy *La Villa Strangiato, 2112* and *Xanadu*.

Peart's shining moment, hardly to be considered simply a "drum solo," was delivered with clinical precision and consummate ability involving complex acoustic rhythms coupled with triggered horn sounds and ending in an homage to the swing-band era complete with accompanying black & white footage of drummers Gene Krupa, Buddy Rich and assorted dancers from "a better vanished time."

Covering so many years' worth of material while trying to make all fans — and themselves — happy in the process is a difficult feat, but judging by the crowd's response it was one which they seemed to achieve. The air-guitar and air-drumming of many audience members was a clear indication of how Rush has inspired many a musician and so it was interesting to get a glimpse into who inspired them as they pulled off powerful covers of *Crossroads* and *Summertime Blues*.

Closing out the night with 1981's *Limelight* seemed a fitting send-off as the celebration of their thirty years in the rock'n'roll spotlight was, for all who were fortunate enough to have been peripherally along for the ride, "the universal dream."

Although I attended other shows both that summer and in 2005, I never gave much more thought to repeating my early-entry efforts. That is, not until the 2006 summer concert season. And following one successful venture refinements in my approach began to take shape — though it was still very much a work in progress.

SEVENTEEN
Journey / Def Leppard

June 23, 2006

You win some, you lose some
— American Proverb

Nearly twenty-five years after first seeing Journey and Def Leppard live, albeit at separate shows, I was making my way to the Tweeter Center where later that evening both bands would be kicking off their first joint tour together. Perhaps as a result of the nostalgia it was likely to evoke in fans like me who grew up in the 80s, as I neared the arena my thoughts went back to when I last saw them in the fall of 1981.

Having only recently released their breakthrough album *Escape* at the time, Journey had yet to experience the chart-topping success it would soon bring them. As such, only two months later they were opening for the Rolling Stones' *Tattoo You* tour with two kickoff dates at JFK Stadium September 25 and 26. With tickets for the second show and it was then that I saw Journey — still with Steve Perry on vocals — for the first and only time.

Touring at the same time in support of their sophomore release *High & Dry* were British rockers Def Leppard. After having seen them at the Spectrum in 1980 opening for Ted Nugent (and the Scorpions on that triple bill), when they came to the much smaller Tower Theater in Upper Darby, PA on October 9, 1981, my friends and I saw it as an opportunity to catch them in a more intimate setting. Still the original lineup and still in a supporting role, this time they were touring as an unlikely pair with southern-rock veterans Blackfoot. That strangeness aside it was a good show — and as it turned out, not only the last time I saw them in concert but also the last time they toured as an opening act. Fewer than two years later 1983's *Pyromania* would catapult them to worldwide success and the big stages would call.

My decision to head to the Tweeter was not with the intention of attending the show, but rather to see if I could repeat my efforts at getting in early as I did for Rush on their *R30* tour two years earlier. Though this attempt was equally deliberate, it was by no means any more calculated or well thought out. I simply arrived at the venue and, to use a fittingly musical metaphor, played it by ear. Although I previously entered by casually passing unnoticed through an office door, this time I was faced with the daunting reality of well-stationed security staff at all entrances. So, dressed in my shirt and tie — work ID again in plain sight — I parked in the horseshoe and immediately slipped into *belonging there* mode as I headed toward an alternate gated entrance.

Approaching the guard, I quickly cobbled together a brief though factually vague story about how I handle transportation services for refrigeration equipment and that the guard at the front entrance told me this gate would be best as it would take me directly to the concession area (as I *am* in the transportation services industry I actually *have* managed refrigeration equipment accounts but had no connection to the Tweeter Center). He confirmed that indeed it would lead to the concession area and without saying any more he opened the gate and cordially welcomed me. I thanked him and continued on to the "business" at hand.

Walking across the courtyard to the doors leading inside, I entered the spacious and familiar atrium; the quiet emptiness once again compelling. Continuing straight across, I entered two more doors that led to the front row at stage left and was exactly where I wanted to be. I immediately scanned the vast and empty house for any signs of authority that might be willing to put a stop to my modest unplanned plan. With no interruptions seemingly imminent I made my way front and center and snapped a few pictures of drummer Deen Castronovo's kit; a predominantly Gloss Black Yamaha set with a double bass-drum arrangement (a rare sight these days as most double-bass drummers now use a double pedal on a single bass drum, eliminating the need for the second drum).

After taking those few pictures, I began to settle in and soon reached a level of comfort that allowed me to continue unwary. As I made my way onto the stage and began poking around at Deen's kit, I encountered his drum tech Jim Handley and introduced myself. We quickly began talking about the kit and during this discussion I asked if he might have a used stick that I could add to my collection. Without hesitation he took one from Deen's stick holder and gave it to me. I thanked him, made some parting comments and left him to continue his work.

Unlike the other sticks in my collection to date, this wood-tipped one is a bit more detailed as Deen has an endorsement deal with New York stick manufacturer Regal Tip (whose founder Joe Calato was the inventor of the nylon tip). Along with an image of the most recent version of the winged Journey logo, it includes the usual manufacturer information: *Journey - Deen Castronovo - Regal Tip by Calato - USA - 7B*.

Both Journey and Def Leppard were sharing the opening and headlining spots on alternating nights of the tour. As Def Leppard drummer Rick Allen's kit was set up on a riser and under a tarp behind Deen's, it was obvious that they were top billing for opening night. After leaving Deen's kit I casually walked behind the risers to get a closer look at Rick's. As Def Leppard's gear had already been set up, there was no drum tech around to approach for a souvenir stick. But I soon found myself in a narrow walkway between the chest-high riser and the backdrop to the stage. So I made my way to his drums and stood directly behind them fixated on all the pedals he had designed to accommodate his modified playing style following the loss of his left arm in a New Year's Eve 1984 car accident.

I snapped a quick picture with my cell phone camera only

to look through the legs of the various drum and cymbal stands to see a stagehand staring at me from in front (I later discovered his name was Rocko). He asked what I was doing as I closed my phone and made my way out from behind the riser. I told him I was a drummer just checking out the set and he rather unpleasantly replied that I wasn't permitted anywhere on the stage. Then he promptly instructed me to leave — which I quietly did as I was still hoping to catch the soundcheck if at all possible. So without one of Rick's sticks I headed out to the seats and waited patiently.

A short while later Rocko and other road crew members took the stage, instruments in hand, and began to tinker around on them one by one as they prepared for what became the pre-soundcheck soundcheck. Once they summoned another of their crew to take the microphone at center stage, they launched into an impressive version of Journey's *Separate Ways* along with a handful of other classic rock tracks in both complete and medley forms.

As I watched rather intently it occurred to me that some of these guys, not unlike many of my former band mates and I, likely had dreams of one day making it to the big stage in their own right. And although not fully realized, it would appear that a compromise had been made with the gods of rock'n'roll somewhere along the line. Though their names don't grace the albums or the tickets for these shows, they *do* get to play on all the very same stages as the artists who managed to grab the brass ring — and that has to count for *something*.

Journey is another band that offers an online opportunity for fans to write show reviews. Even so, having not attended the actual concert, I wasn't able to cover Journey's performance. But I *was* able to review the soundcheck, dubbing the assembled group "The Roadies," and post my review the same day (by 8:20PM EST according to the post notification). I mention the time because given that it was the first night of the tour and that they had only just taken the stage as I was typing; it turned out to be the first review posted (and to no surprise the only one about a soundcheck). I've since wondered if any of The Roadies ever read it:

Although not technically a show review, I did manage

to make my way into the Tweeter Center in Camden, NJ only a few hours ago to catch some of the 2006 summer tour, opening night, pre-show warm-up activity. "The Roadies," as I'll refer to them, did a great preliminary soundcheck covering only *Separate Ways* by Journey. While the song was played well enough for the purpose of initially tweaking the sound board, the vocals were handled by a roadie who was clearly not a vocalist. But considering whose voice he was covering, he pulled it off well enough for this review.

Other tunes, sung by Rocko, included *Rocky Mountain Way* by Joe Walsh, *Dirty Laundry* by Joe's old Eagles partner Don Henley, and a unique version of U2's *With or Without You that* interspersed snippets of songs by The Beatles, The Cars and others before rounding out the medley with the rest of *With or Without You.*

Deen Castronovo's drum tech (wish I had his name) was the phenomenal drummer for the lineup (from one drummer to another - good job mate). His fills and rhythm kept the others on their toes and his abilities in the five-man band were seemingly matched only by Neal Schon's guitar tech — guitarist for The Roadies. Both also seemed to be having fun with their unique gig of playing to a crowd of exactly one — me (with the exception of two sound guys and a lighting guy). At one point the guitarist even began to break into Def Leppard's *Photograph*, a humorous nod to the Brits they're opening for on this summer tour. It was a good set overall which soon led to Journey taking the pre-show stage at about 4:00PM.

Aside from some cool individual warm-ups by each member and a drums-bass-backing-vocals-only semi-rendition of *After The Fall*, Schon, Cain, Valory, and Castronovo (no Augeri) played *Faith In The Heartland* with Cain on vocals and guitar before

I was asked to leave (by none other than Rocko). It seems Journey prefers no one be in the seating area of the arena while they do their sound check. As a fellow musician I respected that and left peacefully. No matter, *Faith'* sounded great, Schon was on fire and the show and the tour seems like it will do well for both bands — which is a great nod to some of the better music to have come out of the 80s.

I just hope this review makes it to the website because even as Jackson Browne knows (listen to *The Load Out*), even "The Roadies" deserve some recognition. Rock on boys…

All in all it was a good day and I was able to accomplish most of what I hoped to, save that one drumstick I didn't get. Oh well… maybe next time.

EIGHTEEN
The David Lee Roth Radio Show

Winter 2006

Having a good discussion is like having riches
— Kenyan Proverb

In early January 2006, following Howard Stern's departure from public radio for the broadcasting freedoms offered by the newer satellite medium, former Van Halen vocalist, solo artist and personality extraordinaire David Lee Roth (Dave) took over Howard's morning slot on a number of stations nationwide. Though short-lived, Dave's talk show encompassed a broad range of topics and he regularly entertained calls from listeners wanting to comment or weigh in with their opinions.

Fun Fact: As a long-time Howard Stern fan I managed to get on the air with him six or seven times during his years on public radio (winning $1,500 along the way). And thanks to Scot in Sacramento I have several of those calls on tape. Because of the time-zone difference the West Coast airing was three hours later than the live

East Coast broadcast. So after each time I was on the show, I'd call Scot and he'd set a tape to catch my call when it played during that later transmission.

~~~

On several occasions, when stirred enough by the current discussion, I would call Dave's show in an effort to express my point of view. Although not always successful in my bid for air time, I was fortunate enough to get through to him twice; both times rather fittingly for discussions that were either directly or indirectly music related. The first topic, appropriately enough, was about Dave and the situation at the time between him and his former Van Halen band mates. The second topic, concerning censorship and how external factors can be an influence on people, had a more peripheral connection to music.

Both calls were interesting experiences as they gave me an opportunity to speak with an artist I've long admired and who fronted a band I've been a fan of since the release of their debut album in 1978. They also provided me a forum to express — to a few million listeners as it were — my long-held opinions about the musical styles between Van Halen and the solo David Lee Roth. Although hardly weighty stuff, when I halfheartedly suggested as such to Kevin — who has quite a few passionate opinions of his own about music — he unapologetically defended both of us quite simply by saying, "It's our *thing*." Exactly! In three words he captured what I knew to be the spirit of this book; no more, no less. Thankfully he also captured digital recordings of my calls to Dave and, as a result, I was able to include the transcripts below.

Content aside, the calls are essentially just another look at moments of artist interaction. And though the means by which these encounters can and do vary, they all share the common thread of my appreciation for all things music.

Call One / January 9, 2006 / Running Time 1m 59s

Dave: Russ, you're here. Number thirteen, speak to me lucky number.

Russ: Dave, how are you doing?

Dave: Extraordinary.

Russ: Great. Hey, I've got a comment about what you just said. You're exactly right regarding changing of the singers. One example, if I can use you… you left Van Halen, or whatever the case was, in '85. Your sound; the sound Van Halen was known for from the first album right up through *1984,* went right with you to *Eat 'Em & Smile.* When *5150* came out? Boom; whole left turn. Not only that… in '96 when the *Greatest Hits* package came out you threw *Me Wise'* on there and you threw *Can't Get This Stuff No More*; two songs that sounded exactly like the old Van Halen, exactly like what David Lee Roth did and sounded nothing like what Van Halen did since your departure. You're exactly right.

Dave: Well Sammy… Sammy maintains that at the age of fifteen he was kidnapped by aliens, and this is true.

Producer: So did L. Ron Hubbard.

Dave: No, that's… he just, he just wrote it. No, no, Sam is uh, Sam maintains that he was kidnapped by aliens. So, routinely, uh this is gonna change his lyric writing capacity. Do ya follow what I'm saying? He's coming from a whole different background there.

Russ: Oh yea, yea, I get it; a lot of his songs contain the word "love."

Dave: So are you saying they shouldn't have gone under that name? You'd change the name, correct?

Russ: Absolutely. And if, you know, it's just you were Van Halen as far as I'm concerned. The sound went with you. A friend and I who were diehard fans for years were just emailing the other day. I made this very point to him, you bring it up this morning, it's just, just perfect timing and I just said, "Man, I wonder," I said to my friend Kevin, I said, "I wonder how much great music they would have put out had that 1996 reunion, you know, continued on. Because based on *Me Wise Magic* and *Can't Get This Stuff No More*... God, those are two killer songs.

Dave: I don't think there was ever any intention to have a reunion there. I think they were just trying to prop up a sagging project there, bring me in and move on to, uh, what inevitably turned out to be another sagging project. I think it's truth in advertising. **(End)**

Call Two / February 6, 2006 / Running Time 2m 46s

Dave: Let's get somebody else to call up and argue with this one, 'cause I wonder if somebody's against all of this. Go for the top there, positive appeal. Russ, you're in, Roth Radio — go.

Russ: Dave, how are you doing?

Dave: Great, my friend. What's cooking?

Russ: Not a lot. Um, I think that, I think uh, you know, part of our human makeup; the characteristics of being an emotional human being is that we're going to respond to pretty much anything, whether it's visual or audible. Uh, hell, if I'm walking past a bakery and I have no inclination to otherwise, uh, have a donut; if I smell something there I might just walk in and grab one. Um, I think everything has some impact on everybody and depending upon what type of person you are, just like the previous caller just said, you know, the bad influences are gonna, are gonna uh, influence the people that are, uh, inclined to be that way and the good maybe, you know, are gonna have the opposite effect. So...

Dave: Okay, but here comes the Bill Cosbys and here comes the Reverend Als and the, here comes a whole variety of people probably on the heels of this latest shooting here, who are gonna start screaming about the lyrical content and then they're gonna start screaming in rage about what's being depicted on the TV set as they have been. But now here's more grist for the mill, more fuel for the fire; what will your reaction be when that happens now?

Russ: Well, I thought that the PMRC back in the, what, the late 80s, took care of that. Did they not?

Dave: Well, the PMRC was a joke that was designed by Al Gore's wife in order to get some kind of a religious right conservative faction interested in their campaign. They were talking about lyrics that were not violent; they were talking about backwards devil messages. They were talking about the kinds of uh, uh, grand guinal I think is what it's called; like monster movies, okay? The kinds of music that they were talking at the Parent's Resource Music Commission hearings in front of whatever that was, Congress or the Senate, was not violent oriented. It was not like hip-hop. They were claiming that it sold satanic messages to our kids. Or that it sold suicidal messages to our kids. Or just, uh, you know, painful drug-oriented messages. Again, I think it was as ill-founded as, uh, contesting what's

	happening lyrically today. But I can tell you there's a huge wave of people that are gonna start showing up in the newspaper on the heels of this latest, uh, routine. Do you think that there should be legislation against rap lyrics because of this?
Russ:	I'm not so sure about legislation, but um, and I haven't maybe thought it through entirely. But I'm not too, uh, in favor of censorship, no. I mean that's a parental thing and I heard again the previous caller talking about, or you, uh, mentioning the, uh, the computer at home and then little Johnny is there in front of the PC. Um, the parental controls are on in my house. I'm very aware of what's going on and hopefully I'm, uh, I'm gonna be effective on a pos—, *in* a positive way with that.
Dave:	Well, that makes you utterly unique. Thank you for calling. **(End)**

NINETEEN
Rush: The Trilogy

July 6, 2007

Part III of Trepidation

Nothing happens unless first we dream
— Carl Sandburg

It was once again a beautiful summer day and Rush was back in town only two months after the release of their eighteenth studio album *Snakes & Arrows*. I had taken off from work in eager anticipation of that night's show and, as such, had no need to be dressed in my usual business clothes. With plans to repeat my earlier successes at gaining pre-show entry, this attire issue presented a bit of a dilemma. Considering it was likely one of the main reasons I previously got in and was able to walk around unrestricted, at the risk of being turned away I had to decide what to do. The options were simple; go as is and bring a change of clothes for later (I didn't plan on leaving once there) or just go casual and see if I could pull it off. After some thought I warily decided on the latter.

~~~~

Fun Fact: This concert was exactly **2** years, **11** months and **2** days after Rush's last show at the Tweeter during the *R30* tour in 2004. *2112* (pronounced "twenty-one twelve") was the title of their 1976 album which sold more than 500,000 copies in the United States; making it their most successful album at the time and breathing new life into their career.

~~~~

Upon arriving at the Tweeter I parked in the "horseshoe" directly in front. This, I discovered, is where many interim workers park while running in and out for various reasons. And as I was once again operating under the pretext that this was all normal and I belonged there, it seemed a logical move as it was well before show time and preparations were still in high gear. I was simply one of many "workers" making use of the horseshoe's easy access.

Stepping from my truck I saw a guard about to close an external gate (the same one I entered before the Journey show a year earlier) after another employee made an inside delivery on what appeared to be a modified golf cart. As he began slowly pulling the gate to a close, I instantly broke into a slow jog and began thanking him for holding it; my gestures intended to give the impression of legitimacy and that, by holding it, he'd be doing me a favor. In sales jargon this is an "assumptive close" — moving forward as if all parties are already in agreement so the prospect will likely to proceed with you. He simply responded, "No problem, buddy!" and let me pass unopposed — my casual look apparently a non-issue.

Once inside I made the familiar walk to the house via the venue's temporary "inner sanctum" and once again saw Lorne onstage hard at work drum teching. A set of stairs on my right led to the stage, so I casually and somewhat confidently took them and headed toward Lorne in an effort to express my gratitude for his kindness during the *R30* tour — *and* to get an up-close look at Neil's new kit. As I approached, I briefly detailed that meeting and was pleased to find him once again cordial. Shaking my outstretched hand he said he recalled the moment well because he seldom lets anyone near the kit when on tour.

As with our previous meeting we again began talking drums — this time about the new Aztec Red and Gold Leaf *Snakes & Arrows* kit. From an aesthetic change to deeper shells on the Roland V-Drums to his concern about flaking of the Black Nickel hardware, he told me it was working out well for Neil; that he was quite pleased with the work of DW (Drum Workshop). Once again not wishing to overstay my welcome, I soon thanked him for his time and headed back to the seats.

Apparently my thoughts weren't yet completely in check as I again forgot to make a plea for a souvenir stick. But only steps away from the riser this time I quickly recovered, backtracked and said, "By the way, I hate to push it but do you happen to have a —" Without missing a beat Lorne finished my question with, "— stick? Sure." He then called me over to a road case to the rear left of the riser and opened it up. Pulling out a pair of Neil's signature wood-tipped sticks he handed them to me saying, "These are from the last show." I later discovered that to be July 4 at the Darien Lake Performing Arts Center in upstate New York — a mere sixty miles southeast of Neil's hometown of St. Catharines in Ontario, Canada.

I thanked Lorne and, walking away, asked about a time for soundcheck. He replied, "It's usually about five o'clock — but you may want to lay low as security may not let you stay for that." Again I thanked him — this time for the advice — and left the stage.

The sticks are the same make, model and size that Neil has been using for his entire career and they're adorned in red print with the latest album and tour info as well as his signature and other standard manufacturer information: *Pro-Mark 747 - Hand-Finished USA - Japan Oak - Rush - Snakes & Arrows - Neil Peart.*

I also noticed another small marking; Neil's initials *NP* in the thick red band which is part of the Pro-Mark logo. As I discovered a few weeks later during a conversation with Michael Lowe from www.neilpeartdrumsticks.com, this mark of distinction is an effort by Pro-Mark to protect fans from purchasing sticks only allegedly used by Neil. To that end it's added only to those sticks provided directly to him and is not on the *Snakes & Arrows* signature model pairs widely available for retail purchase.

For all intents and purposes that was the pair of sticks that reignited the enthusiasm I felt for them more than twenty-nine years prior. Instantly becoming the most cherished of my eventual collection — regardless of others that came before or were to come after — they were a tangible connection to a drummer and band that through their music taught me a great deal about drumming. It was an ideal way to begin any type of collection... with the best piece!

Part II of Trepidation

Before anything else, preparation is the key to success
— Alexander Graham Bell

I decided to put the sticks in my truck for safe keeping, which meant I'd need to leave the arena. But with no desire to call it a day, I needed assurance I'd be able to get back in without issue. So in a twist on the old Wilson Mizner adage: "Be nice to people on your way up because you'll meet them on your way down," I knew it was best to be nice to them on my way *out* because I'd need them on my way back *in*.

When passing the guards at the front door I made sure to engage in some quick and casual small talk, both to get to know them and so they'd get a visual lock on me for re-entry. After a few minutes I said I needed to step outside to my truck, which was within view of the doors. They nodded their approval and off I went.

I placed the sticks completely out of view under my seat and grabbed the 8" clear Tama drumhead and Sharpie pen I brought along in cautious optimism of getting the ultimate autograph — at least for this drummer. Though a simple handshake has more often been preferable to me than an autograph on some random piece of paper, if I was able to get an artist to sign something of meaning to me, something I knew I'd retain and likely display; a book, a guitar — a drumhead — or the like, then I'd make the effort. And this was certainly one of those times — if not *the* time. Carefully tucking the drumhead midway into the back waistband of my shorts and the Sharpie into my pocket, I approached the front doors whereupon a guard kindly opened them for me on sight as if welcoming a VIP to the Four Seasons Hotel. My appreciation extended, I returned to the same seats I was in earlier — section 101, halfway back, right-side aisle — and just watched... and waited.

Nearly two hours passed while I observed the flurry of activity onstage. Setting up various guitar, bass and keyboard gear, rigging lights and sound equipment and even vacuuming the custom-made *Snakes & Arrows* carpet all seemed as choreographed as a Broadway musical. It's often said that "time flies when you're having fun," and that was certainly true for me on this day; my level of interest heightened by witnessing all it takes to put on a concert. Although I arrived early in the afternoon — when most equipment was already in place onstage — in subsequent visits I'd see things from an even earlier phase in the process and be even more amazed at the logistical maneuverings required to make shows like this go off without a hitch (or so it would seem to the uninitiated).

Perhaps even more amazing, or daunting depending on perspective, is that after only a few hours it all happens in reverse, only to continue in this cycle for an entire tour. As Jackson Browne sings in *The Load-Out*; an homage to his road crew: "... let the roadies take the stage, pack it up and tear it down... they'll set it up in another town." Not a job for the faint of heart — or the loath of repetition.

Fun Fact: All the members of bassist-vocalist Geddy Lee's stage crew were wearing t-shirts printed with, "He's Gonna Play the Ricky!" in reference to the old Rickenbacker 4001 bass with which Geddy was so closely associated early on and up through 1980's *Permanent Waves*. Indeed he played it — and to much applause — during *A Passage to Bangkok* from *2112*.

Amid all this hustle and bustle, Neil suddenly appeared onstage with another gentleman; whose name I later discovered was Henry. Casually dressed in khaki pants, a black t-shirt and a baseball cap, he seemed relaxed as he showed Henry, armed with a 35mm camera, around the stage, at one point having a stagehand take a picture of them in front of his drums. Knowing what he has written of his disinclination to be photographed with strangers' cameras, I made what I later discovered was an accurate assessment — that Henry was at least somewhat of a close friend (more about this connection later).

Their appearance only brief, they soon disappeared backstage — an area that I would one day discover holds far more perceived mystique than is justly warranted. This is not to diminish in any way my interest in witnessing all the production goings-on, the musicians dealing with the less exciting side of their jobs and the other miscellaneous activities that go into preparing for a show. But it's just not quite as alluring as is likely thought by most.

With Neil's exit I once again turned my attention to the ongoing preparations and, already well-prepared myself, settled back into a semi-relaxed state of waiting, watching and expecting the unexpected.

Part I of Trepidation

Fear makes the wolf bigger than he is
— German Proverb

Both the waiting and watching proved short-lived as the unexpected indeed occurred when Neil reemerged, effectively nudging me a bit more to attention. During a discussion with some crew members, he began pointing in various directions toward the house. Obviously well outside of earshot, I imagined it having something to do with the sound or the lights or perhaps even the triggered horn and percussion samples so essential to a precise execution of his rather considered drum solo. Something he was concerned with and wanted assurance would be working properly that evening. My conjured-up thoughts aside, the discussion was brief and he appeared to be leaving again — this time toward the front of the stage.

By way of the stairs I had taken earlier that day, he began walking in my direction via the aisle adjacent to my seat. Admittedly, it was a slightly tense moment for me as thoughts ran through my head about how to approach him... or how *not* to.

As previously noted in my letter, he states a similar thought process in his 2006 book, *Roadshow: Landscape with Drums — A Concert Tour By Motorcycle:* "I realized that sometimes it was better not to visit the places of your dreams — better to leave them as exotic, soft-focus mirages of romance."

Yet, here I was about to totally disregard that notion, though I agreed with it to at least *some* extent. But my conflicting view, with which I was undoubtedly about to side, was that implicit in "sometimes" is "sometimes not."

My primary concern was that any advance on my behalf would clearly interrupt whatever he was in the process of doing. He was, after all, "at work" and, as remained in the back of my mind, I was there illicitly no matter how inoffensively. But from a purely physiological perspective I was about to encounter someone I have revered for more than twenty-seven years and, as evident by my concern about the situation, a moment like that is escorted by a certain amount of apprehension.

Having given little thought to how I would seize the moment should it arise, here I was on the verge of a likely once-in-a-lifetime meeting and I was simply going to improvise. As he neared to within earshot I asked if he wouldn't mind signing my drumhead, presenting it to make my request obvious if inaudible. Stopping, he quietly and agreeably said, "Sure," and I handed it to him along with the Sharpie. As he began signing he asked, "Do you play?" I said that I did, introducing myself as I stood up, and he signed in his characteristic way to fellow drummers: *Hello Russ, Happy Drumming — Neil Peart.*

The moment, albeit brief, was absolutely complete with regard to my level of satisfaction and delight; though contained under the circumstances. And in a bit of irony, only after I thanked him and he continued on his way to the FOH sound board did I realize that after nearly three decades as a Rush enthusiast, upon finally meeting him I never even shook his hand.

On his return pass a few moments later I asked if another book might be in the works anytime soon. He motioned toward the stage, arms wide and with just a hint of derision in his voice replied rhetorically, "When do I have time to write a book?" I simply commented that I understood and he continued on and up the stairs.

Taking his place behind the kit for what I hoped would soon be the soundcheck, he began his warm-up shortly before guitarist Alex Lifeson and bassist-vocalist Geddy Lee appeared. Henry had since made his way out to the seats only one row behind me and to my left. And aside from three guys sitting together one section to our left but much closer to the stage, Henry and I were the only others in attendance. Amid the welcome sight and sound of Neil drumming I diverted my attention to Henry for a moment and introduced myself. He responded in kind and when I asked about his connection to Neil he indicated that they're members of the same bicycling club.

Having read all of Neil's works, including abridged online versions of his three privately-published books, I recognized his name as a member of the Western Jersey Wheelmen bicycling club Neil wrote about. Henry was included in 1988's *Pedals over the Pyrenees,* about a cycling trip the club took from Barcelona to Bordeaux. He indicated to me that as a local resident he made arrangements to come to this show and catch up with Neil. I smiled and nodded in acknowledgement but didn't let on that I knew of him from the book, though he told me he was mentioned in "one or two of them" (true as he and the other Wheelmen were also referenced in *Ghost Rider*). Although relatively quiet, he was certainly nice enough. But I was more interested in returning my attention forward not wishing to miss any more of the "private" drum solo / warm-up that was taking place onstage.

~~~~~

Fun Fact: Just prior to the soundcheck a member of the security staff came in from the right side of the house, walked past me and approached the three individuals to my left. Although I was not within earshot, he appeared to be telling them that they had to leave the seating area. Though they pointed out the stick-on passes each had displayed on their shirts, it was to no avail. They were soon heading out and I awaited a similar fate. But upon his return, the guard merely glanced back at me and simply continued on his way. Once again, I could only credit the perceived status of wearing that ID badge.

~~~~~

Following Neil's warm-up, Geddy suggested to the guys at the soundboard (via the PA system) that they replace their cover of *Summertime Blues* with *Distant Early Warning,* or "DEW" as he referred to it, for the next three shows. They then launched into a five-song soundcheck to include DEW, which afforded me the opportunity to see and hear one more song than what the rest of the audience would experience that evening. Membership may have its privileges, but sneaking in has a few perks of its own.

When the soundcheck ended I approached the stage just as Alex began walking across. Meeting up with him at about midpoint, from the front row I asked if he'd sign my drumhead and he agreed, gesturing for me to hand it up. In a less manic state I would have probably chosen to walk onstage and more formally meet him. But caught up in the moment I simply handed it up; thankful he took the time to stop. I offered my Sharpie but he declined by showing me one he had on a lanyard around his neck — presumably ever ready for pesky autograph seekers! He signed and handed it back to me and I thanked him as he went on his way.

With both Neil's and Alex's autographs now on the drumhead, I had to make it complete and, as such, headed for the steps. Once onstage I cautiously moved toward Geddy; not wanting to create a stir. In casual discussion at the time with his bass tech Russ and some others, he appeared to be ready to head backstage. So I seized the moment and approached.

As they all stared with seeming suspicion, I held out my drumhead — hoping the other autographs might allay any concerns and buy me some legitimacy — while simultaneously asking Geddy if he wouldn't mind signing it. With a quizzical look he silently took the Sharpie and signed. I thanked him politely but he said nothing in response; only retaining his puzzled look as he and the others turned and walked away.

Having realized what I consider a rather definitive artist connection (on all counts), I departed — via those stairs, of course — still caught up in the moment yet with all sorts of thoughts running through my head. In their very gracious effort to accommodate my slightly intrusive advances, both Neil and Alex made the memory of those interactions pleasant ones for me. But that fairly awkward moment with Geddy left me feeling a bit uneasy. Assuming I caught him at a bad time; at work as it were, I certainly didn't begrudge him the right to feel infringed upon. And though I was able to savor the moment in its cracked perfection, I was also glad it was over — *and that it was the final one of the day.*

TWENTY
Coming 'Round Again

Arriving at one goal is the starting point to another
— John Dewey

A more active reconnection with music in 2004 prompted me to resume some of the secondary activities I'd dabbled in throughout the years. Having realized some recent "success" in that area, beginning with that Rush *R30* show and a couple of others subsequent to that, it seemed I was once again ready to engage in the lunacy… which further found me more actively enhancing The Collection.

When Kelley and I attended some shows in late 2007 I decided to see what could be done about this reignited interest — and it didn't take too long to find out.

Sheryl Crow

October 19, 2007

You create your opportunities by asking for them
— Shatki Gawain

The first effort was at a Sheryl Crow concert at Caesars Palace in Atlantic City, New Jersey while she was touring in support of her compilation disc *Hits & Rarities*. Kelley and I arrived early, grabbed some drinks and began to settle in when, from my seat, I embarked on a visual tour of the house in an effort to survey my "options."

Fun Fact: Kell and I ended up playing musical chairs at this show, moving closer and closer to the front throughout. Toward the end when a bevy of fans began crowding the aisles at the lip of the stage, Kell got caught up in the moment and joined in — at one point giving Sheryl a "high five" as she reached out to the fans. It was an amusingly proud moment for me as I watched my wife become absorbed in some of the adolescent shenanigans I've taken part in for the past thirty years.

Aware of the relaxed atmosphere at Caesars I took note of the unobstructed and unattended aisles that led to the stage. With the majority of seats still empty I decided to take a stroll down to the front row to get a closer look at the Emerald Green Tama drums as they sat in silence on the riser; the entire stage bathed in a cool haze of mysterious-looking black light — the visual alone suggesting music as actively being played.

Seeing a stagehand casually moving about I quietly called

out to him and he headed in my direction. Mentioning that I was a collector, I asked if he might be able to get a used stick for me from drummer Jeremy Stacey. Though largely unfamiliar with Jeremy's work, I had read enough about him to know of his connection to Joe Cocker, Eurythmics and others.

Without further prodding he happily indulged my request; taking a pair right off the kit as I watched and waited. My appreciation duly extended I returned to my seat showing Kell that my drumstick collection had grown by exactly one pair. And as another first, they were the only ones to date by Massachusetts stick manufacturer Vater. Stamped minimally they included only the drummer's name, make, size and wood type: *Jeremy Stacey - Vater 8A - Hand Selected Hickory.*

John Mellencamp

December 14, 2007

Never separate the life you live from the words you speak
— Paul Wellstone

Nearly two months later Kell and I again saw one of our perennial favorites, John Mellencamp, touring in support of that year's release *Freedom's Road* and playing at the Borgata Hotel Casino & Spa on the Marina side of Atlantic City. Though we had seen him in concert many times in many venues since that first one in 1992, we were just as eager to catch this show.

Fun Fact: Prior to the show Kell and I, along with our twin daughters Alea and Kelsey and my mother-in-law Lynn, had dinner at Bobby Flay Steak in the Borgata. Upon being escorted to our table I noticed

John's wife, model Elaine Irwin (seen on the cover of his *Whenever We Wanted* album) seated with others at a nearby table. After dinner Lynn took the girls back to our room while Kell and I relaxed with a few drinks in the restaurant's casual lounge. Moments later as Elaine walked by, I quietly called out to her. Smiling warmly she took a few steps in our direction seemingly wondering if we knew one another. Quickly putting that to rest with my introduction the three of us spent the next few minutes making small talk about the impending show. Then Elaine and Kell broke into "mom mode" discussing children before, in good grace and at my request, she agreed to pose for a picture with Kell.

~~~~~

The Event Center at the Borgata was a bit more like a typical concert hall, albeit slightly smaller. And it was far less relaxed than Caesars; with security personnel positioned throughout. Despite their presence I was still able to walk unhindered to the front row pre-show to look at the drums and see what my options might be regarding some souvenir sticks.

The first accessible person I came across was a woman with obvious band clout in the form of several laminated passes around her neck. I approached asking if she knew who the drum tech was and she promptly advised me that she was the stage manager, Karen, and asked what she could do for me. I mentioned my drumstick collection and that I was hoping to add one to it from John's current drummer, Dane Clark. Unable to help me at that moment as show preparations were still underway, she said to meet her in front of the stage after the show and she'd see what she could do — even offering her cell phone number in the event that security didn't let me to the front.

Following another fine John Mellencamp show, during which Kell and I eventually made our way to the first few rows (she's getting good at this), we walked to the front of the stage without incident. I half expected Karen not to be available, at least not for some time; assuming she'd be busy with post-show issues both on and off stage. But contrary to my assumption and true to her word she indeed showed up — and far sooner than I anticipated. Fewer than fifteen minutes after the show ended she approached from across the stage holding two sticks — one for me and the other for a woman nearby.

It was another successful connection of sorts and, more impressively, a nice example of selfless integrity on Karen's part. Clutching the non-descript *Vic Firth - American Classic - Metal* stick, I thanked her, wished her well and left with Kell — another addition to my collection in hand.

Fun Fact: During a business trip to Massachusetts three months after this show I made time to visit the Vic Firth Incorporated distribution center in Boston (where I met with Vic's daughter Tracy Firth) and the Avedis Zildjian Company headquarters in Norwell. Both visits had me feeling like a kid in a candy store as there were sticks and cymbals as far as the eye could see. And though my collectible passion is obvious, it's actually cymbals which have long been my favorite component of the drum kit. Although arriving unannounced at Zildjian, I was welcomed warmly by current CEO Craigie Zildjian and her sister Debbie Zildjian, VP of Human Resources — both 14th-generation owners. Craigie provided me a personal tour of the entire facility (save the highly-secure manufacturing floor as time wouldn't permit) to include among other areas a cymbal vault, a specially-designed sound room (where various concert-hall settings can be replicated) and a large drum room where Zildjian-endorsed artists come to test new cymbals. I also saw many notable historical items including a picture of Gene Krupa with Avedis Zildjian III, a framed 1950 handwritten letter to Zildjian from Louie Bellson and, most impressive, a Slingerland drum set given to Armand Zildjian by Buddy Rich the night before he died with the simple request: "Take care of it for me, Armand."

TWENTY-ONE
Taking It to the Next Level

Restlessness and discontent are the first necessities of progress
— *Thomas Edison*

In an effort to build on the success I experienced at these shows in the past few years, I decided to go full-tilt into the 2008 summer concert season with an even more aggressive and to some extent more creative approach. As somewhat of a reminder of my previous disclaimer, when I speak of the creativity used in these activities it's really just euphemistic phrasing for "slightly misleading." But as I have always maintained, these are harmless transgressions — victimless crimes if you will — with no repercussions other than some displaced drumsticks and a bit of fun.

Working off the template I established, or stumbled upon as it were, during my well-spaced efforts in 2004 (Rush), 2006 (Journey / Def Leppard) and 2007 (Rush), I thought a more attentive and inventive approach might net better, more consistent results. By once again adopting more completely the pretense of belonging there, I thought in time and to some extent that may very well come to pass. And so it was that I eventually donned a figurative cloak of duplicity and set out to redefine how I carry out all this foolishness.

Though I maintained this facade for the majority of shows that summer, by season's end I attained a certain fluency in the backstage workings and a blanket of familiarity seemed to settle over me. The frequency of my visits, occasional informed discussions about unloading equipment with the local crew and casual nature with which I carried myself seemed to suggest my being there as valid among staffers and security alike. I slowly lessened my outward though never ostentatious displays of legitimacy and gradually did away with the shirt-and-tie look. And yet from what I could gather, they still seemed unsure of exactly who I was and why I was there — or why I was *allowed* to be there. Short of being misperception on my part (which it very well may have been), it was an interestingly unspoken curiosity on theirs. I was seemingly hiding in plain view — though ever careful not to make waves.

In his memoir *Lucky Man*, actor Michael J. Fox reflects on a similar wariness noting a slight discomfort with his "sudden and outsized" success: "I couldn't help feeling there was something *inauthentic* about the whole thing — if not the situation itself, then at least my position in it. And so in time I began to feel like an imposter. It's almost as if I expected someone, at any moment, to kick in my door and tell me the charade had gone as far as it was going to go."

In time and to varying degrees I would befriend nearly everyone I came in contact with from the guards at the backstage gate to the loading dock crew and a handful of ushers and security guards in the house. And I soon discovered that once I got to know many of them on a first-name basis, my taste for the surreptitious approach I had so carefully cultivated became slightly less palatable. Despite my long-held and previously stated claim that this was all harmless; with respect to those involved there was an element of deceit with which I was no longer completely at ease.

As such, when a certain comfort level was reached on an individual basis, I would confide to some degree my illegitimacy. But admittedly those disclosures were somewhat vague and delivered with a measure of subtlety that lacked the potential blow an all-out confession may have elicited. And in a moment of "self-psychoanalysis" I concluded that it was simply my way of clearing my conscience, however slightly; a way to take the edge off any creeping guilt while maintaining the access I had so "artfully" managed during the past few summers.

Surprisingly, and much to my relief, no one in whom I had confided seemed at all concerned with my acknowledgement. This was most evident by their indifferent reactions, our continued relationships and, most importantly, my uninterrupted backstage access.

TWENTY-TWO
Dave Matthews Band

June 4, 2008

The world makes way for the man who knows where he is going
— *Ralph Waldo Emerson*

First up on the 2008 summer docket at the Susquehanna Bank Center (formerly the Tweeter Center) was the Dave Matthews Band (DMB). Although I was not what would be considered a follower, I knew a handful of their songs and was fond of them. And as any ardent fan or musician likely knows, with regard to musicianship these guys are the real deal; a phenomenal guitarist-songwriter in Dave complemented by an amazing group of guys all no less remarkable in their own right. But the real draw for me was drummer Carter Beauford.

Introduced to Carter's work more pointedly by Kevin, I quickly came to understand what he had long been raving about. Not since my personal discovery of Neil Peart's drumming in 1980 had I been so in awe of the abilities of another drummer. As I said rather emphatically to Kevin shortly after watching Carter's 1997 instructional drum video *Under the Table and Drumming* (a takeoff on the 1994 DMB album title *Under the Table and Dreaming*), "That guy was meant to be a drummer, no question about it!"

As part of my new approach to getting more drumsticks, I began thinking a bit outside the box. Though at this show I was still maintaining the shirt-and-tie look to more easily gain unopposed access to the arena, when it came to getting sticks I thought it best to do my homework. To that end I decided I'd begin finding out ahead of time the names of the drum techs who worked for the drummers whose sticks I wished to add to my collection. Knowing it was unlikely that many people knew who they were I felt it would be better, and in some ways simply more considerate, if I was able to ask for them by name when I approached.

An online search for Carter's tech eventually turned up the name Henry Luniewski, though as part of a story about historic and renovated homes (one of which he owns) rather than for any connection to DMB. But it also mentioned his occupation; displaying a picture of him at Carter's kit.

Upon arriving at the arena I made my way inside through the concession area entrance. A woman, whom I later came to know by name, began to open the large gate just as I was showing her my ID badge and explaining my alleged reason for being there. But before I could do any more than greet her she said, "I don't need any ID; that white shirt is all I need to see to know you're here on business." It seems the power of the shirt and tie had once again paved the way for me; carrying more perceived influence than even *I* thought. But having learned early on to strike while the iron is hot, I quickly thanked her and continued on.

In *Lucky Man*, Fox refers to a similar process: "My strategy was basic: keep moving, *get in and out as quickly as possible*."

The Susquehanna is a typical outdoor amphitheater with reserved seating under a large roof toward the front and lawn seating toward the back. Exterior patios act as both access skirts and eating areas on either side of the arena; off of which are walkways and steps leading to the seating sections. Entry via the walkway, which runs parallel to the stage between the last row of seats and the front of the lawn, provides a panoramic view which lends itself well to my pursuits as a cautious approach must sometimes be considered.

Once inside I made my way across the patio, up the walkway,

to the seating area and down to the stage. From the front row I asked a passing stagehand if Henry was around. He confirmed that he was and invited me onstage to wait by the drum riser — a better waiting area I couldn't imagine — as he went to get him.

Within a moment or two Henry appeared and I introduced myself, quick to point out how I came to know who he was. He was easygoing and freely answered the few questions I asked about Carter's kit; a beautiful Jet Black Yamaha set with a rack system for the cymbals and toms and DW 9000 pedals. I mentioned that aside from being a Carter fan, I was also drummer and stick collector and asked if he might be able to part with a used drumstick. Not sure if he had any readily available, he said I might have to settle for a new one. But after a quick search of a nearby road case, he pulled one out and handed it to me. It had all the usual and preferable dings and dents on the shoulder as well as an unusually worn out and splintered shaft, as if it had been repeatedly hacked by a dull hatchet. This was indicative of connecting often with the snare drum hoop; something with which I have firsthand experience. In a grading system of used sticks, this one would rate near perfect — mostly because amid the centered array of wood fragments were the still-visible signature-series endorsement markings: *Carter Beauford - Pro-Mark Millennium II - Made in USA.*

The summer concert season started off on a good note with a new approach to my modest hobby, a reestablished familiarity with the people of the Susquehanna and a fine addition to my collection. I would take what I applied on this day, refine it as needed, duplicate it and move forward in my Mission to assemble the ideal, for *me* at least, drumstick collection.

Sadly, DMB saxophonist and founding member LeRoi Moore died on August 19, 2008 from complications stemming from an all-terrain-vehicle accident that occurred only twenty-six days after this show. LeRoi was only forty-six years old.

TWENTY-THREE
Tim McGraw / Jason Aldean: Country Gentlemen

June 13, 2008

> *Country music is three chords and the truth*
> *— Harlan Edwards*

The first country artist I ever saw in concert was Tim McGraw during his 2001 summer tour for that year's *Set This Circus Down* album. It was at the Tweeter Center (Kenny Chesney was one of the opening acts) and Kelley and I, along with my sister Kathleen and her husband Jerry, all had lawn seats; or more specifically lawn *blankets*. Though very familiar with Tim's and Kenny's music — and much of country music in general by then — for more than two decades I had been going to concerts of a markedly different style. As such, I wasn't sure what to expect other than something different than what I was used to. I also wondered if I'd be the only one not wearing a cowboy hat.

As it turned out there were far more similarities than differences to the shows I had been accustomed to. Not only did the music rock in a live setting, but an equally rousing energy seemed to emanate from the artists to the audience. The country crowd was cool, engaged and upon closer examination and despite my preconceived notions of appearing as an outsider, not very unlike me. Nestled among the hardcore country fans was an eclectic mix of Rockers and Parrotheads all enjoying this music that, along with its long history and homegrown roots, seems to have borrowed just enough from rock'n'roll, blue-eyed soul and even more recently Jimmy Buffet to be, paradoxically, quite unique.

In 2008 Tim McGraw was back in town with his band The Dance Hall Doctors for his *Live Your Voice* tour. As a fan for several years by then I wanted to add drummer Billy "Thunder" Mason's sticks to my collection, so I made my way to the Susquehanna to see about making that happen.

Arriving late in the afternoon on show day, I entered via the backstage gate and headed straight up the ramp to the loading dock. All the usual pre-show activity was in full swing and I spent a few moments taking it all in, greeting some of the local crew I had gotten to know and in general just getting my bearings, feeling out where and where not to go in an effort to stay out of everyone's way.

Georgia native Jason Aldean was one of the opening acts on the tour and when I spotted a drum tech setting up the kit (a Sonor five-piece in Black and Red Sparkle Fade) for his drummer — as evident by the band name on the bass drum — as usual I wandered in that direction. Introducing myself as a drummer, I launched into the usual litany of questions about drums, cymbals, touring and the like. But I soon decided this guy looked less like a drum tech and more like a drummer. As a point of clarification here, most drum techs actually *are* drummers. But this guy's overall look seemed less "roadie" and more "artist." And when I noticed road cases nearby emblazoned with the name Rich Redmond, I quickly realized that this guy — who introduced himself as Rich — was actually Jason's drummer. He was, in fact, his own roadie.

Confirming this and laughing it off, he told me that it was still a bit early, financially speaking, to have a drum tech on his payroll. He added that it was really no big deal as he only worked "about three hours a day" while on tour anyway. We continued our drum talk and I admitted that although I was familiar with some of Jason's music, I did not yet know who the band members were. But having got to know him, I decided one of his sticks would be well worth adding to my collection and he agreed; pulling one from a road case, signing it and handing it to me. It's a nicely beat-up *Pro-Mark - American Hickory - Millennium II - 5B* model. On it he wrote: *"Russ! U rock! Rich Redmond '08!"*

I thanked Rich and let him get back to setting up the kit. But before leaving I asked if Billy was around as I wanted to meet him as well. He replied that he hadn't seen him recently but would be sure to let him know I was looking for him. As I turned to leave, Billy appeared on the dock and Rich quickly called him over and introduced us.

Extremely gracious, he reached out to shake my hand and actually beat *me* to the questions. I told him of my drumming and stick collecting and that I was a fan of his since getting into Tim's music several years earlier. At that point he seemed determined to give me the Four-Star treatment; asking if I had seen his drums yet, trying to find a stick for me and even offering his business card — the last thing I expected a professional drummer to have. It included all the usual specifics (Billy Thunder Mason / Drummer / Tim McGraw) along with his email address, home address and cell phone number. Needless to say I was surprised, but I accepted it and tucked it into my pocket as he continued to show me around.

Fun Fact: On the way to the stage Billy introduced me to Tim's longtime tour manager, Robert. Upon hearing his strong British accent and taking note of the last name "Allen" on his laminated pass, I immediately thought of Rick Allen; drummer for Def Leppard. I also recalled that a Robert Allen was credited as tour manager on the first Def Leppard album. Feeling confident they may be one and the same, I asked Billy and he confirmed that Robert was indeed Rick's older brother.

Billy walked me to his drums, already set up onstage (and surprisingly behind a Perspex panel — a transparent thermoplastic sound barrier that helps reduce drum bleed), and we discussed in detail the make (DW), his choice of color (Light Blue Sparkle) and his cymbals (Zildjian). Then he took the snare drum off its stand proudly showing me it was his personal Billy Mason "Thunder & Lightning" signature model by Markley. He had a roadie use my phone to take a picture of us at the kit and then invited me to sit at it so he could take a few shots of me playing. Once we were done onstage we walked to his equipment truck as he wanted to find a pair of sticks for me. After a few minutes of searching he found a box of new ones, pulled out a pair and handed them to me. With no manufacturer noted and as evident by the personalized markings they, too, are custom-made: *Billy Thunder Mason - Tim McGraw and the Dance Hall Doctors - www.thunderwear.biz.*

I've been to several country shows since that initial Tim McGraw concert back in 2001 — even having met Carolyn Dawn Johnson, Phil Vassar and Sara Evans along the way (each signing my old Yamaha acoustic guitar) — and each time have found the audience and the artists to be part of a "mutual admiration society." The fans seem to enjoy an all-for-one and one-for-all attitude among themselves and toward the artist. And the artists, in turn, never fail to acknowledge that it's the fans who helped get them where they are. The music, though agreeably uncomplicated and straightforward, actually rocks. And as evident by my exchanges with Billy and Rich, so do the artists (or at the very least the *drummers!).*

TWENTY-FOUR
Maidens, Pearls and Chicago Doobies

Variety's the very spice of life that gives it all its flavor
— *William Cowper*

The remainder of the 2008 summer concert season brought with it an appealing mix of bands and musical styles from heavy metal and classic rock to contemporary singer-songwriters and country. Having grown to appreciate to varying degrees the music of many artists in each of those categories (and then some) during the past three decades; it became a rather exciting, if not busy, summer for me as I diligently and consistently continued on my Mission for those little "cylindrically-shaped pieces of wood."

Although I never tired of this self-imposed diversion despite having attended so many shows — or pre-shows as it were — it certainly had the potential to lose its appeal (as repetition and familiarity are wont to do). And though admittedly I sometimes didn't *feel* like making a special trip to the venue just for the cause, once there I was usually glad I did.

Once again in *Strange Things Happen,* Copeland draws an analogy to fame and its diminishing appeal: "It does lose its fizz, however. If you are an eagle, you're probably over having the world right there on the end of your talons. It's just another day in the boring old sky. And so it was that I tried to remember my most yearning youthful fantasies about the ultimate Olympian state of grace that should be rock star life. When I looked around all I could see was the same old everyday world. Of course, my life was blessed, but why did I have to keep on reminding myself?"

Aside from the obvious benefit of adding to The Collection, I was also meeting new people; crew members and techs who traveled with the bands and who had opportunity to experience the "rock star life" close up, yet almost always with anonymity. Their stories from the road (to occasionally include mentions of their musician "bosses" — though nearly always in a positive light) proved to me another interesting aspect of this behind-the-scenes perspective.

One component that helped stave off any potential monotony was the sometimes drastic change of scenery from one show to the next; and at times in rather quick succession. Elaborate staging, props and pyrotechnic effects for one show would be followed by a minimalist approach for the next. Ten-piece drum sets on eight-foot risers flanked by walls of speaker cabinets would be replaced by a standard four-piece kit on a simple carpet or one-step platform with a few amplifiers scattered about as if set up in someone's living room (but with enough space for 20,000 guests). To see how some bands viewed myriad visual trappings as integral to their live show compared to the polar opposite approach from other bands was a divergence of style that I found intriguing.

Fans at the shows would be equally diverse; each audience reflecting the overall look and style of the band they were there to see. This particular aspect was one with which I could easily identify as I had been attending concerts now for three decades. And in that time I've *been* most of the fans that I see at these shows; the hard rock teen with few responsibilities or concerns, the mid-twenties adult making early strides towards independence and expanding musical horizons and, presently, the middle-aged spouse and parent ("life takes over") seeing bands favored from years past and others more recently discovered.

Though the audiences were fairly well segregated by artist or genre, give or take the occasional overlap; as a whole they were a fascinating mosaic clearly showing that no matter the age group a live connection to music still endures. And given the always-positive atmosphere among those tailgating in the parking lot or interacting with one another inside, it also has a seemingly incomparable uplifting effect on all.

Iron Maiden

June 17, 2008

Caution is the eldest child of wisdom
— Victor Hugo

British heavy metal band Iron Maiden, whom I hadn't seen live since 1981 at the Tower Theater, had one of the more theatrically-adorned stages of the summer when they brought their Egyptian-themed *Somewhere Back in Time* tour to the Susquehanna. A ceiling-high backdrop depicting their longtime horror-influenced mascot Eddie as an Egyptian mummy was the centerpiece around which all other embellishments were displayed. The stage itself was decked out with oversized Egyptian sarcophaguses, Basenji dogs (one of the world's oldest breeds; drawings of which had been discovered on the walls of ancient Egyptian tombs) and a thirty-foot tall mummified Eddie in tattered rags (which, in keeping with heavy metal's image, I later discovered shot sparks from the eyes). The setlist noted that seven of sixteen songs would include pyrotechnic effects and, as with all shows where they were used, a representative from the local Fire Department was on hand to assure there were no safety code violations with their use.

Fun Fact: During a conversation with the Fire Inspector onsite that day, I discovered he was a long-time fan of Iron Maiden and had tickets for the show that evening. Although there on official business at the time; he was thrilled to be getting a behind-the-scenes look, taking pictures as he simultaneously did his inspection and in effect playing a small part in the overall process of the show. And as an example of the audience overlap I mentioned, he would be returning later that evening... with his teenage son.

~~~~

When I asked Iron Maiden drummer Nicko McBrain's drum tech about getting a used stick he was quick and apologetic, "Sorry, I don't have any..." But as I was standing behind the drums at the time (a marble-finished, Light Blue DW set with an Egyptian pattern) I clearly saw several sticks in a bag hanging off the floor tom as well as one or two on the tom itself. Discretion being the better part of valor — and by extension the better part of these activities as well — I decided against pointing it out ("you win some, you lose some"). Erring on the side of caution — or etiquette as it were — proved wise as he continued, "...but I can give you a new one if you want." Pulling one out of the bag, he handed it to me and I accepted, politely thanking him for what became the latest addition to my collection; a *Vic Firth - USA - Nicko "Boomer" McBrain* signature model.

Pearl Jam

June 19, 2008

Simplicity is the glory of expression
— Walt Whitman

The first example of a quick and dramatic shift in stage scenery occurred only two days later when Pearl Jam was in town on their brief and simply-titled *2008 U.S. Tour* - even the name reflective of their unpretentious approach. Their setup was equally straightforward; the most ornate visual being a striking stage-wide backdrop of the painting *The Great Wave off Kanagawa* by Katsushika Hokusai; an eighteenth-century Japanese artist known for works representing the masses.

According to Professor Witold Kinsner from the University of Manitoba, Canada: "Hokusai placed the common man into his woodblocks, moving the emphasis away from the aristocrats and down to the rest of humanity."

Perhaps this choice of background was pointedly deliberate — less about the art and more about the artist's intention to celebrate the common man.

Regardless, gone were the massive displays and elaborate accoutrements from forty-eight hours prior and in their place, simply enough, were the tools of the musical trade; drums, guitars, amplifiers and microphones. As always, of course, the literal and figurative center of attention for me was the drums. Former Soundgarden drummer Matt Cameron's five-piece set of Natural Birch Yamahas — one of the most appealing finishes I would see all summer — was situated center stage on a low-level riser and complemented nicely by an array of gleaming Zildjian cymbals.

Fun Fact: One of my early and more enduring musical memories occurred on Christmas day 1979 when I awoke to find a brand new Zildjian 16" Medium Crash cymbal under the tree. My excitement unrestrained I immediately ran to my kit and replaced my old no-name, beat-up crash with the beautiful new one. Although my drumming was still in its infancy, I discovered a new appreciation for sound, tone and *beauty* in cymbals that to this day has not waned. Soon after, when I had saved enough money, I bought a new set of Zildjian 14" New Beat hi-hats and once again went directly to my kit to play "out with the old and in with the new."

As I approached to get a closer look I met up with Matt's drum tech, Neil, at the riser. After a quick introduction and my customary (and always enjoyable) few minutes of drum talk, I broached the usual topic of possibly getting some sticks. His lighthearted — but valid — response was, "What's in it for me?" Without missing a beat and thinking of nothing else offhand, I offered to get him something to eat and drink if he wanted. But he was quick to reply that he was only kidding; almost apologetically adding, "I can get food and drinks in catering." I then pulled out some gum for myself and handed a few pieces to him as well — which he seemed to appreciate quite a bit. Although it was a simple common courtesy and not an effort at paying it forward, he said, "This is the first time anyone *gave* me anything — they usually just *ask* me for stuff when they see me working onstage."

I admitted to him that although it was not intended as a bribe (I'd be hard pressed to think a few pieces of gum would suffice) it was indeed the first time *I* offered something in one of these situations as well. Of all the techs, musicians, stagehands, guards and other assorted staff I've met over the years (to include the driver who walked me through singer Eddie Vedder's tour bus following a conversation we had in the backstage lot), I never thought I had anything of value to offer *them* other than casual conversation and a genuine interest in what they do. But his words made me think and, as such and regardless how modest it seemed on the surface, from that point forward I decided that gum would be the ice breaker; a kind yet simple offering to my fellow Planet Drum inhabitants who assisted me in these efforts.

He then motioned for me to follow him to his work-station road case (already open and exposing a pair of lime-green-and-white Adidas sneakers he said Matt wears when playing) where he pulled out a pair of used sticks and handed them to me. In keeping with Pearl Jam's unassuming theme, they, too, are simply adorned: *Vic Firth - USA - Matt Cameron*. I thanked him for the sticks, he thanked me for the gum and with a slightly new perspective I was soon on my way — another Mission accomplished.

Fun Fact: In a sign of the times on many levels Pearl Jam made an effort to "go green" on this tour by partnering with Verizon Wireless to allow fans to purchase paperless "mobile tickets" — the necessary information for admission stored on their cell phones. In conjunction with this partnership they were also aligned with the National Network to End Domestic Violence (NNEDV) and had a tour bus and trailer in the parking lot (clearly marked as Live Mobile Bootleg Recordings) offering concert goers a free download of their choice from one of three songs from that night's show in exchange for donating no-longer-used cell phones.

Chicago / The Doobie Brothers

June 26, 2008

Classic art was the art of necessity
— Max Eastman

Classic rock was fairly well represented during the 2008 concert season by various bands from the 60s, 70s and 80s. But within this genre were two that, aside from touring together, clearly personify and rank among some of the *most* classic both by longevity and uniqueness-of-style standards — Chicago and The Doobie Brothers.

With multiple Top Ten hits between them and having collectively sold more than one-hundred-fifty million albums since arriving on the scene in 1969 and 1971 respectively, both bands have stood the test of time, weathering not only the inevitable obstacles of personnel changes but the myriad shifting musical tastes of an often capricious public.

It took The Doobie Brothers until their second release to experience the widespread success Chicago enjoyed almost immediately (although interestingly the self-titled debut album by The Doobies, as they're more casually known, contained a song titled *Chicago*). When 1972's *Toulouse Street* netted two hits, *Listen to the Music* and their cover of the Arthur Reid Reynolds song *Jesus Is Just Alright* (previously recorded by The Byrds in 1969 and Underground Sunshine in 1970) the band began a long and successful run with twelve original studio albums, most of which have attained gold or platinum status and a total of seven Top Ten hits.

Fun Fact: As previously noted the very first 45-rpm record I bought soon after discovering music was The Doobie Brothers' only number-one hit *What a Fool Believes* from their only number-one album, 1978's *Minute By Minute*. And in one example of the artist crossover that's always intrigued me; Chicago's drummer Tris Imboden came to that role from Kenny Loggins' band. Kenny and former Doobie Brothers' keyboardist-vocalist Michael McDonald co-wrote *What a Fool Believes* — each recording a version with their respective bands. Kenny's version is on his 1978 album *Nightwatch* — on which Tris played drums.

As one of very few bands with dual drummers it was only fitting that The Doobie Brothers would provide an opportunity for a dual addition to my collection — the first and only such opportunity I would get. Longtime drummer Mike Hassock, who initially joined the band in 1972 only to leave two years later and then return in 1987, and newer recruit, former Vertical Horizon drummer Ed Toth, were the current percussive lineup.

Although Ed played a standard four-piece DW kit in a Ruby Glass Sparkle finish, Mike was the first professional drummer I had known to play DW's specialty line of Short Stack drums (in a beautiful Rich Red Fade over Maple finish). Short Stack drums are shallower than traditional drums and, although sound is subjective, in comparison they're said to provide an alternate studio and live sound as the shallow chambers, or shells, offer a full round tone with more open resonance and sustain. As with any other instrument the tenor of a drum can vary based on myriad factors. And whereas the visual arts consent that "beauty is in the eye of the beholder" (Margaret Wolfe Hungerford in *Molly Bawn*), I offer my own tongue-in-cheek twist on that as applied to music — and to drummers in particular: "Beautiful sound is in the ear of the beat holder." (Groan)

As I approached both Mike's and Ed's drum techs, atypically during a slightly busy pre-show moment, I was quick to state my case and step aside in my continued effort never to be a hindrance ("always harmless, never disruptive and all in good fun"). No usual drum talk, no ice-breaker offering of gum; just some quick pleasantries, a request for sticks and a hasty retreat. But despite all my circumstantial concerns both techs were quite pleasant, each agreeably indulging my request quickly but without any evidence of annoyance at my imposition. As with so many other techs I've met during the past few summers and despite whatever stereotype may exist about "roadies" in general, by and large my experiences with them have all been quite positive.

Just as with Mike's kit, so, too, was his stick different as it was the first jazz one to join my collection. Made — or "turned" in drumstick terminology — from hickory, jazz sticks are typically thinner and lighter, designed for the faster, more fluid movements of jazz drumming. And judging by the way it's worn with nicks and splinters on the butt end, he apparently plays them backwards (as some drummers are known to do for various reasons). A well-worn signature model, it's actually bowed in the middle from either wear or weather: *Pro-Mark Jazz Made In USA Texas - Doobie Brothers - Mike Hassock*. Ed's is a signature model as well but unused, pristine and bare (no lacquer finish as on most sticks), offering the first Kelly-Green ink printing of any stick I had seen up to that time: *Pro-Mark - Made In USA - Hickory - Doobie Brothers - Ed Toth.*

Chicago's debut release, *The Chicago Transit Authority,* was a bold and unusual start for any band — a double album. But that boldness was soon validated when the album produced three hits in *Does Anybody Really Know What Time It Is, Beginnings* and

Questions 67 and 68; all three eventually becoming radio staples and live concert favorites. By the time their second album was released they had simplified their name to Chicago in response to threatened legal action by the actual Transit Authority of Chicago. Ever since, they have continued unabated recording twenty original studio albums —several of which have attained gold or platinum status — and garnering more than twenty Top Ten hits along the way.

I first saw Chicago at the Spectrum in late summer 1984 and quickly became a casual yet admiring fan. Having seen them a handful of times since, I've come to respect both the studio and live work of former session drummer Tris Imboden, who was recruited in 1990 when founding member Danny Seraphine was let go. And when they came to town this summer, I saw a nice stick opportunity and decided to seize it.

Tris' drum tech John, whom I approached at the riser as he was tuning the kit, was one of the older techs I had met but was as kind and appreciative of my "fellow drummer" status as any of the others. As such, he indulged me as I asked my questions — in this case about Tris' uniquely bowed rack system and what appeared to me to be a swirling wood grain on his shells. He informed me that the rack was designed specifically for Tris by hardware manufacturer Gibraltar and the shells were a new offering by DW called Twisted Exotics. Made from rare poplar trees found in France, the grain runs diagonally around the shell as opposed to the more standard vertical run.

Following our brief discussion, and upon my usual request, John was happy to contribute to my collection a nice pair of used sticks right out of Tris' stick bag. They're personalized with his name and the band's logo: *Vic Firth - USA - Tris Imboden - Chicago.*

One show, two bands, three additions to my collection — a "classic" day in every sense of the word. Variety indeed.

•••••••••••••••••••••••

TWENTY-FIVE
A Mötley Festival of Singers, Songwriters, Priests and Eagles

It takes all sorts to make a world
— *English Proverb*

An array of artists, offerings and audiences continued into midsummer with an eclectic mix of bands and solo performers — some old, some new and one still alive and well since its 1994 renaissance of sorts when Hell apparently froze over. Suffice it to say there was something on the calendar of events for most rock'n'roll fans who were — fittingly and equally — old, new and still alive and well.

John Mayer / Colbie Caillat

July 10, 2008

Blues is easy to play, but hard to feel
— Jimi Hendrix

Although John Mayer had already been serving up his mellow brand of acoustic-heavy pop and blues-tinged rock since 2001, he was still largely viewed as a newer artist, at least compared to most others who came through town that summer. And though I was only a casual admirer familiar with his more well-known work, it was by way of the Zildjian cymbal website that I became aware of his touring drummer J.J. Johnson (who also performed on the studio track *Only Heart* from John's 2003 release *Heavier Things*). So I decided his stick would be a nice addition and headed to the venue to see if I could make that happen.

Soon after arriving and entering via the backstage gate, I made my way past the tour buses and equipment trucks, up the ramp, across the loading dock and out to the stage where I encountered J.J.'s drum tech at the riser. Following a brief discussion about the simple Ludwig kit and how the tour was going so far, upon request he kindly handed me a gently-worn Elvin Jones signature model stick — the second jazz one I'd receive: *Pro-Mark Millennium II - Jazz - Made In USA - Hickory - Elvin Jones.* Elvin was an accomplished and influential jazz drummer from the post-bop era of the early-to-mid 60s and worked with Miles Davis, John Coltrane and many others including — coincidentally — a jazz trombonist named J.J. Johnson.

Opening for John was the more recently discovered Malibu, California singer-songwriter Colbie Caillat. Her blend of pop, surf and blue-eyed soul in combination with the allure of her dusky contralto vocals seemed the perfect female complement to John's musical style and, as such, an excellent addition to the tour. No stranger to the music world, Colbie is the daughter of record producer Ken Caillat, best known for producing and engineering three Fleetwood Mac albums including 1977's *Rumours*, for which he won a Grammy Award. As would be expected, Ken co-produced both of Colbie's releases.

As a combination of session and touring musicians make up her band both in the studio and on the road, I was unfamiliar with who might be playing on this tour. But when I met the drum tech setting up a kit on a riser on the loading dock (many drum kits are set up back there and then rolled into place making the band transitions easier and quicker) he informed me that her touring drummer, who doesn't appear on either CD, was a guy named Mike Baker.

He eagerly discussed the kit and answered some questions I had about the cymbals when I noticed the unusually large hi-hats (15" as opposed to the standard 13" or 14"). After our conversation I figured I may as well add one of Mike's sticks to my collection too. Though I never heard him play nor was he a noted or endorsed artist (only standard markings on his stick: *Vic Firth - USA - Hickory American Classic - 3A*), if nothing else its inclusion can be viewed as a "tour set" — headliner and opening act — as I have it displayed along with J.J. Johnson's.

Mötley Crüe

July 12, 2008

Life is a festival only to the wise
— Ralph Waldo Emerson

Rock'n'roll festivals have been around at least since the Monterey Pop Festival took place at California's Monterey County Fairgrounds in June 1967. As rock'n'roll's answer to the long-running Monterey Folk Festival, which has been held there since 1957, it was an effort by promoters to validate rock music as an art form and is generally looked upon as one of the first manifestations of the "Summer of Love."

More commonly known as rock fests, the large-scale, multi-act, usually single-show outdoor concerts typically run anywhere from one to three days. And although countless such events in many forms have taken place all over the world in the years since Monterey, only a handful of them have put their stamp firmly on the history of rock'n'roll. Some of the more noteworthy ones are Woodstock (NY) in 1969, California Jams in 1974 and 1978, Knebworth (UK) in 1979, US Festivals (CA) in 1982 and 1983, Live Aid (PA and UK) in 1985 and the Moscow Music Peace Festival in 1989.

One offshoot of these festival shows has been the creation of benefit concerts which are planned annually, typically with a varying lineup of artists within a particular genre and in an effort to raise awareness and funds for social and environmental causes, healthcare, poverty relief and human rights efforts. Farm Aid, spurred on by comments made by Bob Dylan during his appearance at Live Aid, was organized to assist farmers throughout the United States and is one of the more well-known and successful of these festivals having generated more than thirty-five million dollars since its first concert in 1985.

Fun Fact: One of the first benefit concerts on record was held on December 28, 1791 for the family of Austrian-born Classical composer Wolfgang Amadeus Mozart following his death of uncertain illness-related causes at age thirty-five. Many prominent musicians of the day attended the benefit and performed Mozart's works in his honor.

In yet another spin-off of the festival show, the touring rock fest has come into vogue in recent years. As with the one-time and annual versions, this adaptation maintains a multi-act roster of similarly-styled bands — typically with one as the headliner — and tours several cities during each concert season. Some notable touring rock fests include alternative music's Lollapalooza, heavy-metal's Ozzfest (initially created as a two-day festival when Lollapalooza organizers refused to let Ozzy Osbourne join the tour) and Lilith Fair, the all-female festival created by singer-songwriter Sarah McLachlan in response to the lack of concert and radio attention she felt was being paid to female artists. Although there are differing accounts, Lilith is identified in biblical literature as Adam's first wife and is considered a symbol of strength and independence as she refused to submit to his authority, leaving Eden for parts unknown.

If necessity is the mother of invention then, as Ozzy and Sarah have clearly proven, exclusion must be the mother of innovation.

Although many of these events have causes associated with them, others are organized and promoted for the simple enjoyment of the music itself. One such festival, according to its creator, Mötley Crüe bassist Nikki Sixx, was designed to bring "bands that embody the spirit of rock'n'roll" to the masses. And so it was that on a hot and sunny Saturday in July the Crüe Fest circus came to town; their proverbial tent poles raised high at the Susquehanna.

With five bands on the bill (Mötley Crüe, Buckcherry, Papa Roach, Sixx A.M. and Trapt) and all the accompanying visual trappings to be expected from such a hard-rock and heavy-metal roster, the show was another example of the stark contrast between genres. In reverse order this time, the simplicity of the John Mayer show from just two days prior gave way to a far busier atmosphere both on and offstage. The backstage lot had several tour buses, equipment trucks and, in a sign of the times, a large enclosed tent complete with tables, chairs and zebra-striped carpets amid a full array of Rock Band gear all set up for play.

After a brief look inside the tent I headed in my usual direction and encountered four large drum sets — one for each supporting band — all set up on risers on the loading dock. Onstage I noticed all the visual frills as anticipated; in this case an assortment of large video screens, erratically-shaped microphone stands (fashioned from pipe and looking as if they were run over by a truck) and one graffiti-covered baby grand piano, among other odds and ends. The largest accouterments were the lighted letters, each one ten-feet tall, six-feet wide and intentionally facing backwards. They read right to left across the entire stage and spelled "Los Angeles" in a nod to Mötley Crüe's most recent release, *Saints of Los Angeles*.

Amid the chaos of the stage crew setting up everything from band equipment and lighting rigs to stage monitors and pyrotechnic effects, I managed my way to the drum riser where Tommy Lee's DW kit was already in place. Not quite what I expected, it had an exaggeratedly oversized bass drum (approximately 40" and simply for show) that was situated at the front, hiding most of the kit from audience view — including the actual 24" bass drum. The drums were a surprisingly minimal mix of floor toms and two gray electronic trigger pads in place of any mounted acoustic toms. An alternate electronic chrome snare sat to the left of the hi-hats and a marching-band bass drum was angle-mounted to the left of that. All acoustic drums were a translucent red, with the exception of the primary snare in a brass finish. And in another first for me, I noticed all the acoustic toms, including the 24" bass drum, had exterior drum triggers mounted to them. When affixed to the drumheads of acoustic kits they convert the energy produced by a stick attack into electrical impulses, effectively transforming the acoustic drums into electronic drums.

Two techs were tending to Tommy's set; one his personal tech (William "Viggy" Vignola) and the other a local crew guy assisting with the more cosmetic tasks; shining the cymbals, drums and hardware. Viggy, a large and intimidating presence with several earrings, a shaved head and tattoos enough to rival the well-inked Tommy, was actually quite easygoing and nice. But given the hectic atmosphere I skipped the drum talk, opting instead to simply introduce myself and ask about a souvenir stick.

Pulling one out of Tommy's stick holder he showed it to me and explained that they're not typical wood sticks. They're a more expensive composite of aluminum and polyurethane made by Ahead; the top half of which can be replaced when worn out. He then handed it to me and said he doesn't often give them away because they're not disposable. But he'd make an exception this time. I thanked him as I tucked it into the back pocket of my shorts and made some small talk with the local guy before stepping out from behind the kit, off the riser and heading out the backstage gate.

This signature model stick was another first for my collection as the only non-wood addition to date; with a black aluminum grip and a gray polyurethane shaft it's stamped *Ahead - Made In USA - Tommy Lee Studio - 16.63 STS - Tommy Lee.*

(The) Eagles

July 14, 2008

Sometimes all you have to do is ask
— Randy Pausch

Beginning auspiciously enough as Linda Ronstadt's 1971 backup band (even playing on her self-titled third album the following year) the original lineup of the Eagles saw quick success following the release of their self-titled debut album in the summer of 1972. In the wake of hits *Take It Easy, Witchy Woman* and *Peaceful Easy Feeling* they helped to popularize the Southern California country-rock sound while simultaneously becoming its very epitome.

But an acrimonious breakup in 1980 seemed to be the final chapter in the Eagles' rock'n'roll story; an ending perhaps best illustrated in the liner notes of their final offering, *Eagles Live*, that states in whole, "Thank you and goodnight." And as co-founding member and drummer-singer Don Henley said at the time about any possibility of a reunion; it would happen "when Hell freezes over." Though it took nearly a decade and a half for that unlikely climate condition to materialize, in early 1994 the Eagles launched their aptly-titled *Hell Freezes Over* reunion tour. And in a lighter moment while addressing the obvious during one of the recorded shows, co-founder and guitarist-singer Glen Frey was quick to joke, "For the record we never broke up; we just took a fourteen-year vacation."

Fun Fact: Glen Frey was said to have always been adamant that the group not be referred to as "The Eagles," but rather just "Eagles." To that end none of their studio or live albums ever had the adjective "The" before Eagles — although it does show up as such on a couple of later compilation releases.

The enormous success of that *Hell Freezes Over* tour and the equally well-received live album of the same name brought the band a renewed success and has kept them busy for the better part of the past sixteen years. When they released their seventh studio album *Long Road out of Eden* in late 2007 and announced a supporting tour for the following year, Kelley and I as well as Kevin, his then-girlfriend Kelly and some other friends all made plans to go.

Seeing the Eagles live in 2008 would distinguish them as the band I had waited longest to see — thirty-six years — and in that time both they and the world saw many changes. The year *Eagles* was released, record albums were granted U.S. copyright protection for the first time, NASA announced the development of the Space Shuttle program (which is scheduled to retire in 2010) and Richard Nixon won re-election as President of the United States. And on the same day that their debut album *Eagles* was released, June 17, five men were arrested for breaking into the Democratic National Committee headquarters thus beginning the infamous Watergate scandal which eventually led to President Nixon's resignation from office.

Arriving early at the Wachovia Center we stopped for a few drinks in one of the spacious concourse bars before heading into the house. Typically restless in these concert situations, I excused myself a few minutes before the others to head inside for all the usual reasons. Thankfully, we had floor seats which made getting down to stage level easy (and for once legitimate). After scouting out our seats I headed toward the stage as the thousands of other fans filed in from all sides, searched for their seats and began the wait for show time.

As I made my way toward the front, a man standing behind the front-row barricade dressed in black with an indiscernible laminated pass hanging around his neck became my focus. Once there I politely waved him over and, introducing myself, asked his name (Tony) and whether he worked with the band or the arena. His good-natured reply of "the band" allowed me to continue easily, making some brief small talk and telling him that I collected drumsticks — my usual segue into The Question. Just as I was about to ask, he gestured for me to wait a moment and disappeared behind a black curtain draped around the lip of the stage. Assuming he had business to attend to I patiently waited, watching the stage crew make their final preparations. When he reappeared a few minutes later, much to my surprise he had a pair of sticks in his hand. He casually handed them to me with a simple request that I not tell anyone where I got them (he said he'd prefer not having to fend off additional requests all night). I easily agreed, thanked him for his generosity and headed to my seat to wait for the others.

The ease with which this particular Mission played out reminded me of a story told by the late Carnegie Mellon Professor Randy Pausch in his 2008 book, *The Last Lecture*. Wanting to ride in the front car of the monorail while at Disney World with his son and father, his father said he didn't think it likely. But Pausch replied that he once learned a "trick" to getting what you want in life, and he promptly asked the attendant if they could ride up front. The attendant replied, "Certainly, sir." Pausch then turned to his father saying, "I said there was a trick; I didn't say it was a *hard* trick... sometimes, all you have to do is ask."

Though I was well aware that drummer Scott Crago had been part of the Eagles backup and touring lineup since their reunion, I wasn't sure whose name, if any, would be on the sticks as Don had been their drummer since the beginning. And given his obvious status both within the Eagles and as a solo artist, I was quietly hoping it was his endorsement. But either way I knew a pair of Eagles sticks would make a nice addition to my collection and, as such, was quite satisfied with the following markings on the nicely-used pair: *Vic Firth - Eagles - 2008 - Scott Crago.*

Judas Priest

August 6, 2008

There is moderation even in excess
— Benjamin Disraeli

As with shows by Iron Maiden and Mötley Crüe earlier in the summer, British heavy metal band Judas Priest did their sort proud by adorning the stage with all the visual trappings their audience was surely expecting. As headliners on that summer's festival-like Masters of Metal tour (with Motörhead, Heaven & Hell and Testament), included in their display were multi-tiered platforms with ornately "sinister" frills situated throughout, a nearly ten-foot high drum riser and a stage-wide backdrop with a fittingly oversized and overseeing likeness of the 16th-century French prophet Nostradamus emblazoned across it — an image taken from the cover of their 2008 double album of the same name. Even the Harley Davidson motorcycle that singer Rob Halford has long been known to ride onstage was there, though still in an equipment truck (into which, of course, I ventured for a closer look).

Fun Fact: The term "heavy metal" was first used in print by writer William S. Burroughs in his 1962 novel *The Soft Machine* when referring to one of his characters as "the Heavy Metal Kid." It took on more of a musical allusion in 1968 when it was included in the lyrics: "I like smoke and lightning, heavy metal thunder" from Steppenwolf's seminal hit song *Born to Be Wild*.

But unlike the others, Judas Priest; their name taken from Bob Dylan's 1967 song *The Ballad of Frankie Harding and Judas Priest*, was a pioneer of the style. Forming in 1969 and preceded only by Germany's Scorpions (1965), fellow Birmingham natives Black Sabbath (1967) and Hertford, England's Deep Purple (1968), they're one of only two heavy metal bands to have played at Live Aid — the other being Black Sabbath, who, along with original singer Ozzy Osbourne, reunited for the event at the behest of organizer Bob Geldof. And though some categorize Led Zeppelin (1968) as one of the first heavy metal bands; attaching that label to them has long been an issue of debate given the divergence of style and substance between them and those more decisively of the genre.

According to Led Zeppelin guitarist Jimmy Page in Stephen Davis' biography of the band, *Hammer of the Gods: The Led Zeppelin Saga*, "We were never a heavy metal band, we were hard rock. It's a bastard term to us. I can't relate that to us because the thing that comes to mind when people say 'heavy metal' is riff-bashing, and I don't think we ever did riff-bashing at any point. It was always inner dynamics, light and shade, drama and versatility that we were going for."

I first became aware of Judas Priest in 1979 when they opened for KISS at the Spectrum on the *Dynasty* tour — otherwise dubbed the "Return of KISS." On the tour in support of their 1978 album *Hell Bent for Leather* (titled *Killing Machine* in the UK but renamed for release in the United States to appease the Columbia/CBS Records executives who disliked the "murderous implications" of the original title), Judas Priest was at the time beginning to experience more mainstream success. And though friends and I became casual fans soon after that show (another on the menu of musical "fast-food"), with the exception of the Live Aid performance Kevin and I saw, we only caught them live one more time when they headlined a Tower Theater show on July 31, 1981 following the release of their seventh studio album, *Point of Entry*.

As I arrived at the Susquehanna on the opening night of the tour I quickly noticed that the backstage lot was crowded with an unusual number of tour buses and equipment trucks — perhaps to have been expected given that four rather established bands were on the bill. As such, the loading dock was equally unusually packed with drum risers, road cases and crew members all going about the business of making the show happen.

Onstage, however, things were a bit less crowded — though no less busy. And in those conditions I simply assumed a low profile; opting to observe all the hustle and bustle from a distance while waiting for a moment of calm to approach the drum tech. Occasionally I'd pass the time by chatting with other techs as they restrung instruments or otherwise did their mostly stationary work — which was more amenable to discussion than some of their more itinerant responsibilities. Most were just as sociable as the drum techs and I believe it was my active knowledge of music coupled with a genuine interest in their work that lent itself well to those discussions. It was also in part why so many of them spoke seemingly without restraint about the good, the bad and the ugly of life on the road.

Every so often in my stage travels I'd come across items other than drumsticks that were of collectible interest to me; guitar picks, setlists, drum heads and the like. But on this day it was a stack of backstage passes sitting openly on a road case. Some were orange, others yellow and all potentially granting at least some level of access. Picking up a yellow pentagon-shaped one with "Priest Feast Europe 2008" printed on it (apparently left over from the recent European tour which, I later discovered, continued with a second leg in early 2009), I quickly deemed it worthy of inclusion in my collection of memorabilia and tucked it away in my pocket.

Longtime drummer Scott Travis, with the band since 1989, had a chrome-finished, eight-piece, double-bass DW set (though he had long been endorsed by Tama drums). Situated on a riser nearly ten feet above stage level, his kit was one of the few I wasn't able to view up close that summer. But I *was* able to approach the drum tech and, introducing myself, tell him of my interest in adding one of Scott's sticks to my collection.

Though no used ones were available, he was quick to hand me a new one adding that this *Vic Firth - USA - Scott Travis - Judas Priest* model (the only one I've seen with a red — not white —

nylon tip) was not available for purchase thereby making it — at least in the context of this hobby — *somewhat* rare.

I accepted the stick and the information and, amid the continued pre-show preparations, was soon on my way unable to remain for the show (as would be the case many times this summer).

TWENTY-SIX
Toby Keith / Montgomery Gentry

August 16, 2008

Uncertainty and expectation are the joys of life
— William Congreve

This would mark the tenth time I attended either a show or pre-show during the 2008 concert season and it turned out to be, quite by chance, a turning point in my ongoing look inside the engine room of live music. Inadvertently pushing the limits of access, not by doing something more but rather by omitting a step in the usual process; I discovered that hiding in plain view *onstage* worked just as well as *offstage*.

In support of their respective recent releases, *35 Biggest Hits* and *Back When I Knew It All*, Oklahoma native Toby Keith (born Toby Keith Covel) and Kentucky duo Montgomery Gentry were on the road together for Toby's *Biggest & Baddest* tour when they made their stop at the Susquehanna. A fan of both artists for a few years by then I set out on a beautiful, sunny late Saturday afternoon to check out what would be the second of only two country shows I would attend all summer.

Once inside, and following the usual exchange with the

local crew and staff, I made my way to the stage and, as always, immediately headed toward the drum riser. Quickly noticing that Toby's drummer Dave McAfee's drums — another nice set of Natural Birch Yamahas similar to Matt's from Pearl Jam — were already set up, I turned my focus to the rather unique riser.

If it wasn't obvious that Ford Motors was sponsoring the tour by the "Built Ford Tough" slogan and logo emblazoned across all the equipment trucks and at various points throughout the stage, it was certainly evident by Dave's drum riser which resembled an oversized chrome front bumper; complete with a proportionately large and familiar Ford emblem. And in what would prove to be an enduring sponsorship, not to mention an ongoing theme of tour names and stage sets, the riser on his follow-up *Bigger & Badder* tour in 2009 would resemble the tailgate of a truck; complete with another Ford emblem and a mock license plate reading "Big Dog" in a nod to the nickname Toby earned following the release of his 2007 album and song, *Big Dog Daddy*.

For the most part this was a typical pre-show setting; stagehands going about their business in every direction, techs setting up equipment at their respective stations and the FOH guys doing their thing from the cordoned-off section midpoint back in the seats. Perhaps the only unusual aspect up to this point was that despite being in the midst of all these people and all this activity, I had yet to encounter Dave's drum tech, Lance.

By the time the stage cleared for the crew's dinner break I gave up on that notion and decided to take things into my own hands, quite literally, by grabbing one of the nylon-tipped sticks from the stick bag hanging off the floor tom. Though not a used one, it is an endorsed *Vic Firth - USA - Dave McAfee* signature model and, as such, would do fine in my display.

I would later connect with Lance telling him of my earlier pilfering at the drum riser (all for the Mission, of course) and, with good grace, be summarily let off the hook. It seemed that being a drummer and stick collector in some way came across as a legitimate or respected enterprise with the many drum techs I encountered and as a result they were willing to suffer my impositions, accommodate my requests and, on the rare occasion, pardon my infractions.

The onstage atmosphere during dinner breaks always intrigued me and whenever the opportunity arose I'd soak up these unusual conditions in quiet contemplation; either lost in thought about what it would be like to be the performer on that stage or wishing Kevin or Scott was there as both have similar interest in this "other side" of the music. The stage, clear of any crew members, was completely quiet and actually quite peaceful. The entire house; from the stage to the seats to the farthest reaches of the lawn, was in a veritable state of sleep as the workers fueled up in catering and the occasional security guard or usher relaxed in any one of the more than 7,000 seats. A sort of calm before the storm settled over the entire place, oddly enough creating an atmosphere in stark contrast to everything a concert hall typically represented — and which it would become in very short order.

Soon after the crew returned, Montgomery Gentry took the stage for their soundcheck. It was during this time that I turned the corner from merely collecting a stick or two and disappearing to more fully and closely experiencing the pre-show activities. I essentially took it to yet another level simply by not leaving — something I had only done twice before (excluding that 1995 Van Halen soundcheck at the Spectrum); though even those moments were from the relative safety of the seats.

As the band members strapped on guitars, stepped up to microphones and, in the case of drummer Tony Hammons, took a seat behind the drums — a double bass, Red Sparkle set of Ludwigs — I remained onstage. Stepping onto the riser I introduced myself in the usual manner and, without further comment, he quickly pulled a used stick from his bag, asked his tech for a Sharpie and signed the *Vater Xtreme Design - XD-5A* wood-tip stick to me (complete with his rendering of a little snare drum and sticks): *"Rock On! Thanks — Tony Hammons."* We then took a picture together at the kit and discussed drums and technique at length — perhaps more than with any other drummer or tech I had met. He showed me a few rudiments of his pre-show warm up and as the soundcheck was about to begin, invited me to remain on the riser throughout.

As they rolled through *Back When I Knew It All* and *Something To Be Proud Of* with only Troy Gentry at the microphone, co-singer Eddie Montgomery noticeably absent, I closely watched Tony's playing, occasionally glancing out at the rest of the band and in general taking it all in from yet another, even more powerful perspective — onstage and at the drums.

When soundcheck ended I took a picture with Troy, said goodbye to Tony and headed for the backstage exit. As I made my way down the loading dock ramp I crossed paths with an unusually hatless Eddie as he was about to board their Montgomery Gentry and Jim Beam-emblazoned tour bus. I introduced myself, mentioned my fondness for the lyrics in *Something To Be Proud Of* (he thanked me though I knew it was written by Jeffrey Steele and Chris Wallin — as are many of their songs), shook his hand and continued on my way.

It was a good day; a pivotal day, and I would take my newfound "bravado" (or perhaps audacity) and apply it to future shows as tactfully and unobtrusively as possible as I continued my look inside the world of live music.

TWENTY-SEVEN
Kid Rock / Lynyrd Skynyrd: Southern-Fried Rock

August 22, 2008

Life is the sum of all your choices
— Albert Camus

Upon first hearing that Kid Rock and Lynyrd Skynyrd were touring together and would be coming to town, I marked the date on my calendar without any pressing interest in going — either for sticks or the show. But as the date drew closer I began to think about all the music I liked from both artists — even if only casually — and how that had always rated in my assessment of whose sticks I wanted to include in my collection.

Of course Lynyrd Skynyrd's music has been part of the American rock'n'roll landscape since their first release, *Lynyrd Skynryd (pronounced 'lĕh'nérd 'skin-'nérd')* back in 1973 and I quickly became familiar with all of their Southern-tinged, blues-rock hits after discovering them.

Kid Rock, born Robert Ritchie, was a far more recent discovery having made his musical entry more than two decades later and merging into the world of rock'n'roll after a start as a hip-hop rapper from Romeo, Michigan just north of Detroit. In one of the more unusual and successful genre-blending efforts of any artist in recent times, his wide-ranging abilities took him from breakdancer to hip-hop DJ (where club goers' comments of "that white kid can rock" earned him his stage name) and from rapper to rocker where he further blurred the lines of classification by fusing hard rock, southern rock, country and pop.

And so it was that late in the afternoon on a hot and sunny Friday I found myself heading over to the Susquehanna, chatting with the crew members and wandering around onstage just as Kid Rock's backup band, Twisted Brown Trucker, was about to perform their soundcheck. With the memory of the previous Saturday's Montgomery Gentry visit still fresh in my mind I remained onstage, albeit safely off in the stage right wing, and watched the set — sans Kid.

As soon as they were done, I approached drummer Stefanie Eulinberg as she headed in my direction, introduced myself and asked if I could add one of her sticks to my collection. As the only female drummer I would meet in all my backstage adventures and as she had played on all Kid Rock albums since the breakout 1998 release *Devil Without a Cause*, I was glad to have made the effort to show up that day. But surprisingly she didn't say yes, although she didn't say no either. And though we were only fifteen feet from the riser; one of the sticks she just used during soundcheck sitting in plain view on the snare drum, she said to check back with her after the show and she'd see what she could do. With that we shook hands and she continued on her way.

Once she was gone I approached her drum tech, Mark, introduced myself and told him I was a stick collector. And in one of those more direct moments of occasionally using "mild deception" to carry out my Mission, I told him that Stefanie said I should check with him about getting a used stick. Without further question he turned toward the Gold Sparkle set (the only Gretsch drums I'd see all summer and now under cover to shield them from audience view before show time), grabbed that stick from the snare and handed it to me. We shook hands and I thanked him, quick to disappear from the scene of the crime in the event that Stefanie was to return.

As the first (and only) stick I would get from a female drummer, similarly it's the first (and only) one that has a gleaming, chrome-like finish (Silver Optic as it turns out) which reflects light, creating a rainbow effect around the stick like stripes on a candy cane. Unevenly worn near the wood tip it's one of the more detailed and customized ones I'd receive: *Vater Color Wrap - Hand Selected Hickory - Power 5B - Kid Rock - Stefanie - Twisted Brown Trucker.*

Returning from my truck, where I placed the stick for safe keeping, I again made my way to the stage to see what the opening band, Lynyrd Skynyrd, had going on in the stage and drum departments. As opposed to not knowing too much about Stefanie, I was well aware of drummer Michael Cartellone, both from his nearly ten years with Skynyrd and from his time with Damn Yankees in the late 80s and early 90s; both of which made his stick a worthy candidate for my collection.

Casually taking in all the onstage hustle and bustle, I soon noticed his drum tech (Kyle Davis I would later learn) working on the mostly-complete, six-piece set of Pearls — the only white set I'd see all summer. As I approached, and in this setting what amounted to a rare moment of diverted attention from the drums, something else caught my eye — he was wearing a Rush *Caress of Steel* tour t-shirt.

When meeting drum techs for the first time the ice breaker of choice (aside from the surprisingly well-received gum) is typically a casual introduction followed at some point by The Question. But the opener this time was more a reactive and unrelated question: "Is that shirt from the actual tour?" Looking up from the business at hand and in a reply indicative of both fan and kindred spirit, Kyle said almost disappointedly, "No — but I wish it *was*!" We hit it off from that moment and I was once again pleased with my decision to head over that day. In one of the more relaxed, natural and lengthy conversations with any drum tech to date, we soon arrived at the introduction and continued on with a discussion about our fondness for Rush, about drums in general and even about his personal experiences with the upside of life on the road… and the downside of its toll on relationships.

I discovered that we're the same age, that he's from Columbus, Ohio (near my friend Dan) and that he's been teching for several years with many different drummers, Frankie Banali (Quiet Riot) and Robert Sweet (Christian hard rock band Stryper) among them. As he's also a fan of the NHL Columbus Blue Jackets, I connected him with Dan (who worked for the team at the time) and he was able to get him tickets to a few games once Kyle returned home from the tour. We exchanged phone numbers and email addresses and still occasionally connect to catch up with one another.

Of course, I eventually asked about a used stick and, though he didn't think he had one available at the moment, he quickly located one in a nearby case and gladly gave it to me as the latest addition to my collection: *Pro-Mark Millennium II - Made In USA Hickory - Michael Cartellone - Skynyrd.*

Unfortunately, only five months after this show on January 28, 2009, longtime Lynyrd Skynyrd pianist (and former roadie for the band) Billy Powell died of an apparent heart attack at his home in Orange Park, FL. He was only fifty-six years old.

TWENTY-EIGHT
Journey / Heart / Cheap Trick: Stage Right

August 26, 2008

Every historian discloses a new horizon
— George Sand

As the door was about to close on yet another concert season, I attended one last show in late August and found myself taking a few more liberties than anticipated (or thought possible) when I began all this silliness of poking around where I didn't belong.

Although gone were most of the cautious, defense-mechanism jitters that accompanied my earliest efforts, merging even further into the pre-show activities by remaining for a few recent soundchecks restored a few front and center; even if only short term. And as they carried with them moments of apprehension and excitement in equal measure, I held fast to my low-profile rule throughout. But following a few of those ventures the contentment that settled in became a sort of restlessness; a desire to experience more — and to get those mirror neurons firing once again.

As the progression of this modest thirty-year diversion

came about in what may be considered just the right order — better seating, backstage access, an assortment of drumsticks and watching a few soundchecks — it stood to reason that if it was to continue it would do so in much the same way — logically. And as it became gradually more inspiring at each interval, I pressed on; each of those steps collectively giving way to the next (logical) one — remaining for some of the shows (or more specifically — *onstage* for them). Just as with a TV show's season-finale teaser; this night would close out the summer with a taste of things to come — and perhaps a remedy for my restlessness as well.

Since the release of their self-titled debut album in 1977, Cheap Trick has averaged a new release every two years; placing them among the most consistent recording and touring bands in rock'n'roll. And as more than twenty-seven years had passed since I last saw them in concert, I was eager — and due — to catch them again as they promoted *Rockford*; the 2006 album recorded in and named for their Illinois hometown.

My first stop was the loading dock where I met drummer Bun E. Carlos' drum tech, Matt, just as he began setting up the standard four-piece set of Green Sparkle Ludwigs. Following a brief discussion about how he came to his position after leaving a more traditional "shirt-and-tie job" in Chicago, we began talking drums as he pointed out some of the finer details of the kit — notably Bun's signature inside the snare shell (apparently he signs all his snare drums; this one dated May 2008) and the fact that he only plays virgin bass drums (no tom mounts attached).

I was also drawn to the double-typed, triplicate Cheap Trick logo on the front of the bass drum — a visual that brought back memories of that first show nearly three decades before. I also noticed a small pink and white rabbit — or *bunny* as it were — sitting on top of the bass drum. Though the connection wasn't immediately clear, within a beat or two I picked up on the humorous nod to his name and came to the conclusion that the otherwise conservative-looking drummer must have a healthy sense humor.

My turn of the discussion to a drum stick request was initially met with apprehension as Matt noted that Bun doesn't typically like to give them away. But before I could tell him to forget about it, he grabbed a used one from the nearby stick bag — a *Pro-Mark - Made In USA - Millenium II - Bun E. Carlos* signature model — and handed it to me. I thanked him and after a few more minutes of small talk, let him return to his business at the kit while I wandered off to another part of the dock, another tech and another set of drums.

On my way, however, I noticed guitarist Rick Nielsen standing with his tech (Paul) in front of two large open road cases; each revealing an array of guitars — many of which I recognized immediately. Standing just a few feet away and well within earshot, I was in no particular hurry and, as such, opted to casually wait as they discussed which guitars to use, how well their concert t-shirts were selling and where the next show was (Bristow, VA). In the familiar stage garb he's long been known for — a dark suit, white shirt, bowtie, hat and sneakers — Rick was taller than I expected and quite nice; my casual "hello" met with a pleasant reply as he headed down the ramp toward the backstage lot.

At that point I approached Paul, introduced myself and asked about some of the more well-known guitars displayed before us. He readily answered all my questions and, as with Matt, eagerly shared stories of how he got into the business and which other bands and artists he's worked with along the way (Alice Cooper among them). Though to some extent he appeared quiet, his affability surfaced in conversation and proved him to be one of the most easygoing guitar techs I'd meet all summer. This would later factor in to how the night would progress. But for the moment I left him to his teching as I refocused on that next drum riser.

Though new releases from Heart have been few and far between in the past decade (2004's *Jupiter's Darling* being the most recent as of this visit), they've always maintained a consistently active touring schedule — often behind compilations or live releases. And this time around it was a bit of both as *Dreamboat Annie Live* was released in late 2007 and *Playlist: The Very Best of Heart* in 2008. But new material notwithstanding, and as it would be the first Heart show under my belt, I was pleased I'd finally be able to see them.

As with all multi-band shows, the loading dock was jammed with drum risers, road cases and sound equipment all being pushed and pulled in various directions by crew members who daily live by the old showbiz adage: "The show must go on." And to that end Heart drummer Ben Smith's drum tech Jeff was hard at work doing much the same as Matt and Paul; taking care of his little corner of this rock'n'roll world.

As he was just getting started on Ben's kit, I introduced myself but kept the discussion brief. And in what came naturally to me — lending a hand and drums — I began to assist by setting up a few stands and handing some cymbals to him from an open road case. Thanking me he started to open up about details of being Ben's tech for the past nine years and about his recording studio in Heart's hometown of Seattle.

Sharing some of my own story in response I mentioned The Collection and in a welcome twist on my usually having to ask, Jeff offered to contribute. As he began digging around in a road case marked "Heart Upstage Center Drums," I pointed out my preference for used ones "if any are available." Though this may seem a bit demanding, even suggesting the expression "beggars can't be choosers," in my experience most techs immediately reach or search for a new one; perhaps thinking — in a reasonable assumption that the nicest equates to the best — that I'd prefer a pristine stick for display. But for my purposes quite the opposite is true; the more dings and dents a stick has endured at the hands of its owner, the more character it has and, consequently, the more inherent value.

Although lacking much of the aforementioned character, at the very least the barely-used one he found for me fell under my category of firsts as the only Zildjian stick I received to date. Simple in design and markings, it's a wood-tipped signature model and stamped: *Zildjian 5B - Select Hickory - USA - Ben Smith.*

Happy to accept it I thanked Jeff and set out toward the stage on my third and final pursuit of the day. In ice hockey vernacular when a player scores three points in one game it's termed a hat trick — so named in 1967 when Montreal's Henri Henri hat store used to reward such players with a free hat. If successful in this final pursuit, I would pull off a sort of *triple* hat trick — three sticks from three drummers in three bands... at one show. Cue the bells and whistles.

Despite several lead vocalist setbacks; arguably the most difficult issue for a band to remedy without experiencing a substantial dwindling of the fan base, Journey managed to remain together and fairly active over time. Within the span of a year, from June 2007 to June 2008, they found a new frontman in Filipino singer Arnel Pineda (in a sign of the times — via YouTube), released ten new songs on a double album of new material and re-recordings (*Revelation*) and launched a headlining tour. And aside from that partial soundcheck in 2006, I hadn't seen them fully in concert since 1981.

By the time I ventured out onstage nearly all of their gear was set up, to include drummer Deen Castronovo's double-bass, Gloss Black Yamaha kit with the *Revelation* winged logo on the front of both bass drums. As such, I didn't expect to see his drum tech — at least not right away. But while I was admiring the set from in front he came walking out from backstage offering a casual nod and a wave as he began tending to some minor details on the riser.

I introduced myself in the usual way (name, drummer, stick collector) and he replied in kind (Steve Toomey, drum tech, drum builder). It was that last part that intrigued me most as I was always curious about the other side of drum teching — what these guys do when they're not on tour.

As it turns out, most remain connected to drumming in one way or another. While some go on to tech for other well-known bands, teach private drum lessons or work in recording studios, others move to the working side of the kit and play drums in their own bands. As for Steve, he's co-founder of NorCal Drumworks and spends his time building custom-made drums in California (when not playing in his band) and lists Deen as one of his customers and drum teachers.

After some discussion about drum building and his touring work with Journey, I asked about a used stick for my collection. He countered with an offer of a pair which, aside from the purple grip tape, was essentially the same make and model as the one Steve's predecessor, Jim Handley, gave to me back in 2006. Along with the Journey logo and a much larger manufacturer name they were the same wood-tipped, black-stamped, signature model: *Journey - Deen Castronovo - Regal Tip by Calato - USA - 7B*. I thanked him as we both walked backstage and parted on the loading dock.

~~~~~

Fun Fact: Although I would occasionally visit catering for food and drinks throughout the summer (sometimes bringing bottles of cold water out to the parking attendant who always let me in), this was the first time I had dinner with some of the local and band crews before a show. Invited by one of the guys on the dock, over a meal of chicken, fish, potatoes, vegetables and a drink I listened as they told stories of their summer on the job. It was just another dinner break at the office for them — but a bit of interesting insight and "research" for me.

~~~~~

I soon reconnected with Paul stage-right as he tuned Rick's guitars on what I discovered was a typical workstation for most guitar and bass techs — a few road cases opened to reveal a fold-out table and drawers for all their tools of the trade. And just as with those of us in the more conventional workforce, so, too, do many techs adorn their work spaces with various photos and other items of personal interest. I've seen pictures of girlfriends, wives and children as well as stickers, passes and countless other effects collected from their years on the road. Many have mentioned to me the importance of keeping that area at least somewhat personalized as it offers occasional moments of clarity for why they're out there away from their home lives for extended periods each summer.

We talked as he tuned and shortly before the 7:00PM show time, he welcomed me to stay for Cheap Trick's set. Without hesitation I accepted and settled in on a nearby road case to watch from the wings. Within minutes he was strapping a guitar on Rick, the show was underway and I was sitting in perhaps the best seat I've had in thirty years of going to concerts.

In her memoir, *High on Arrival*, actress and sometimes-musician Mackenzie Phillips; daughter of John Phillips from the legendary 60s group The Mamas & the Papas, reflected on similar occurrences. Though a sense of entitlement seemed to be the upshot for her (quite contrary to my simple appreciation of the moment), she captured the experience well in few words: "I'd perch sidestage on a road case, sauntering backstage to refresh my drink. I got spoiled — who wanted to go to a concert if you had to sit in the audience?"

Although opening to a half-empty house, Cheap Trick played as if in their heyday; a tight and energetic eleven-song set enhanced for me by proximity which, in turn, created a heightened sense of connection (especially when Robin Zander ambled over to where I was sitting during a verse in *Surrender* and again when Rick tossed a handful of picks at me as I snapped a few shots with my cell phone camera). But before I knew it the final notes of *Dream Police* were ringing in my ears as Rick handed his guitar to Paul and ran past me, disappearing through the backstage doors.

Though that first front-row occurrence in 1981 was exciting, it was no match for this first onstage experience — both coincidentally for Cheap Trick.

As the sun went down the seats filled up and in the burn of twilight Heart took the stage. My seat remained the same and once darkness fully descended the view took on a more concert-like feel making my first Heart show more intense than I would have anticipated. The ten-song set included mostly hits and two well-known covers (The Who's *Love Reign O'er Me* and Led Zeppelin's *Going To California*).

Seeing the band huddled together in the darkness only moments before taking the stage and witnessing Nancy's quick guitar-change technique between songs were just some of the behind-the-scenes advantages from my perspective. And as my "seat" was very near Nancy's guitar tech's workstation, at one point I offered him a piece of gum and he said, "Nice — thanks!" handing me a couple of guitar picks in exchange (although my offer was again just a common courtesy). After *Crazy On You,* the final of two encores, Nancy feigned the need for yet another guitar change as her tech laughed and turned away before she, too, retreated backstage.

Between bands and amid the hectic and fast-paced transition from Heart's gear to Journey's, I left my spot to stretch and see what might be going on backstage. It was there that I spotted Journey founding member and bassist Ross Valory alone on the loading dock smoking a cigarette, so I approached. Shaking his hand I introduced myself and, as he appeared almost happy to have company, I took the opportunity to ask a few questions:

Me: So, how's the new Steve doing out there?
Ross: He's just amazing — everyone who hears him is blown away.
Me: That's cool… and how about the tour?
Ross: It's going great! But it beats up the audience a bit.
Me: How so?
Ross: It's a long show; Cheap Trick gives them forty-five minutes, Heart does an hour and we give them ninety minutes. But it's definitely a good bang for the buck.
Me: Yea, I saw those set-times on the schedule. I'll let you go — and I'll see you out there. You're on Jon's side, right?
Ross: No, Jon's on *my* side!
Me: Right — I'll tell him you said that if I see him.
Ross: You do that.
Me: Nice meeting you.
Ross: You too — enjoy the show.

As he walked down the ramp toward the buses I returned to my stage-right seat and watched the ongoing preparations. But right when the transition was complete I was asked to leave the stage unless I had a pass. Just as in 2006, Journey's security was keeping a tight rein on any outsiders during soundcheck.

So I made my way backstage toward catering where I passed Deen as he was warming up with some light drum rolls… on some guy's upper back. A somewhat strange practice method that I assumed was more spontaneous than usual. But either way there he was right next to me as I watched for a moment but said nothing. I then ducked into catering to grab a drink and plot my next move. When I came out only a few minutes later they were already onstage playing and I was surprised by how faint the sound was that bled into the backstage area.

Rather than leave I decided at this point to watch the show

from the seats and headed from the loading dock to the open concession area through the nearest set of doors and out to the front row… where I stood for exactly one song. When I couldn't produce a ticket for a guard, again I was asked to leave. Quickly finding a corporate box about halfway back with about ten seats in it — all empty — I happily settled in. My contentment, however, was soon interrupted by a passing guard.

When asked again to validate my seating, once more I came up empty — just as another security guard happened by. As the first one began explaining the situation while simultaneously shining his flashlight on me, the second quickly cut him off and was told not to worry about me. And as I sat back in my seat; once again content, beneath the din of the show I offered a hushed "thank you" and waved to Ron — the head of event security — whom I had come to know well during the summer. He returned a "no problem" nod, waved back and continued on.

A picture of the setlist taken with my phone allowed me to know what songs were coming next and, ultimately, when to leave to beat the inevitable mass exodus. As it had already been a long and productive day — as this sort of thing goes — I opted to leave early, closing out the summer with three bands from the halcyon days of my youth, adding three sticks to my collection and taking this quiet hobby to yet another level.

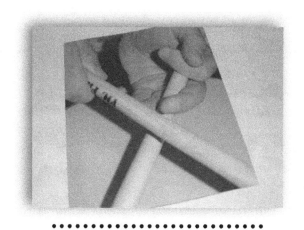

••••••••••••••••••••••••

TWENTY-NINE
Putting Down the Sticks

*The mind ought sometimes to be diverted
that it may return to better thinking
— Phaedrus*

Although I had been attempting to chronicle these events while simultaneously attending all the shows and pre-shows (and tending to myriad other responsibilities along the way), my notes continued to pile up quickly as the more exigent task of getting the stories down suffered a much slower pace.

This backlog of experiences and information began to weigh on me with regard to a self-imposed though somewhat shifting deadline and I realized that attending shows — gathering more grist for the mill as it were — was an ironic contributor to this dilemma. The exasperation that resulted found me reflecting on advice received decades earlier from my mother. Whenever I'd get frustrated while working on something, she'd simply say, "Just put it down and come back to it later."

As a young drummer experiencing similar moments of restlessness when attempting to learn a difficult piece, she would again offer her advice, albeit with a slight twist: "Just put down the sticks and come back to them later."

Though I certainly appreciate the music of The Beatles, I've never been what would be considered a devoted fan. But to this day whenever I hear *Let It Be* I'm taken back to one of my earliest and strongest connections to music. I was very young when I first heard it but recall an immediate and deep fondness; very aware of the reference to Paul McCartney's mother (Mary — my mother's given name) and how the opening verse and chorus aligned so well with my mother's ongoing advice:

> *When I find myself in times of trouble*
> *Mother Mary comes to me*
> *Speaking words of wisdom*
> *Let it be*

Accepting and applying this advice both to drumming and to other areas of my life proved positive on many occasions. And in the midst of this particular project, I once again found myself turning to it as I attempted to arrive at more of the actual *writing* in my writing.

Just when I needed a break from the seemingly incessant information gathering, the end of the concert season was upon me offering a welcome respite; an occasion to let it be — to decompress, organize notes and thoughts and continue my writing relatively uninterrupted.

That is, of course, until it all began anew the following summer.

Part III:
EVERYTHING AFTER

*It's just a phase that I'm goin' through
But I don't wanna change it*

DOES SHE KNOW / 1986

THIRTY
Bruce Springsteen: The Spectrum Revisited

April 29, 2009

There's nothing half so pleasant as coming home again
— Margaret Elizabeth Sangster

As with last summer's efforts to take these adventures even further, to explore and see more with each visit, the 2009 summer concert season (which actually began in the spring) started not at the Susquehanna but rather the Wachovia Spectrum. Although I hadn't seen a concert there since October 30, 2001 when WMMR hosted an anniversary show featuring Isle of Q, Fuel, David Lee Roth and The Hooters, having spent my "formative" concert years there in effect laying the groundwork for all this nonsense, it was somewhat of a homecoming for me.

With the recent (and initial) announcement that the Spectrum would be closing for good in late 2009, Bruce Springsteen was almost immediately named as one of the final acts with a two-night stand slated for April 28 and 29. Interestingly, it would be a sort of homecoming for him as well as it was the site of his first arena date as a headliner back in the early 70s. As such, and as Max Weinberg's sticks were on my collection radar (if for no other reason than he was a fellow New Jersey drummer), I headed over early in the afternoon on Day One.

Fun Fact: In late 1974 after auditioning for and being awarded his role in Bruce Springsteen's E Street Band (the name derived from the Belmar, NJ street where an early rehearsal space — the boyhood home of original keyboardist David Sancious — was located), Max's first public appearance was at the Main Point in Bryn Mawr, PA. The small coffeehouse boasted a Who's Who of famous performers over the years and would also be where Bruce and the band played the first live performance of *Thunder Road* under its original title *Wings for Wheels* (taken from the lyrics "... to trade in these wings on some wheels...").

Managing my way into employee parking just outside the arena I entered via an open concession delivery door and quickly made my way to the lower-level seating area behind the stage (or where the stage *should* have been). I took a seat at the far end of the house to survey the landscape as crew members assembled stage, light and sound equipment; all of it as I had never seen it before with countless chain hoists hanging from the ceiling to the floor, speaker cabinets lining the boards and the stage opposite where it is during performances. Even the fly tower; the rigging area usually high above the stage, was on the floor as crew members prepared it for show time.

Looking out at the 18,369 wine-red seats in the forty-two-year-old arena brought back a veritable lifetime of concert memories and I took it all in as if having discovered a long-lost photograph from my youth. Whether general admission (unreserved) seating as in the early days or reserved seating (as with all shows following The Who's December 3, 1979 concert tragedy at the former Riverfront

Coliseum in Cincinnati — incidentally promoted by Philadelphia's Electric Factory Concerts), I was able to pinpoint where I sat for the majority of shows I attended. And as the memories continued to surface I was reminded how music — and all its connections — has such a lasting impact on our lives.

As Levitin (*This Is Your Brain on Music*) points out, lower brain functions analyze physical features and higher brain functions work to integrate them into a perceptual whole. In correlating the lasting effect of these images to music (and vice-versa) he states that "what we see and hear is the end of a long chain of mental events that give rise to an impression, a mental image, of the physical world."

After reasoning that there was no way the band's equipment would be set up any time soon, I made my way to the loading dock where a crew member confirmed my suspicions. And although it never dawned on me before; he also mentioned offhandedly that the Spectrum — with its single-bay loading arrangement — is not very well liked among his fellow roadies. Whereas most arenas now have loading docks with room for multiple trucks, the Spectrum's accommodations only allow one at a time leaving many workers waiting around which, in turn, makes their pre- and post-show efforts much longer than they need to be.

With this news of a sluggish load-in I decided to leave, opting instead to return the following day when the gear would already be set up and when there would likely be far fewer people to duck and dodge. And upon my late afternoon return on Day Two, as suspected it was similar to occasions at the Susquehanna; empty, quiet and actually quite peaceful — the drums silently though impressively perched high on their riser overlooking all other instruments as if king of some inanimate musical realm. Musically speaking, especially from a drummer's perspective, it was a rather moving scene.

Having again entered through the concession doors, I took the same path to the lower level, this time continuing down to the floor behind and under the massive, three-tiered stage. Asking for Harry McCarthy, Max's drum tech of many years, a crew member summoned him via two-way radio and we were soon introduced. After some small-talk about his Drum Paradise business as well as his tech work with several other notable drummers, I arrived at The

Question and he was quick and eager to contribute.

Completely devoid of any identifiable markings (another first), the sticks are "custom made for Max by Regal Tip and are between 5A and 5B in weight and size," according to Harry. He also noted that they were from the previous night's show — what *was* to be the next-to-last one at the Spectrum.

Fun Fact: Pearl Jam hosted the final public event at the Spectrum as part of a four-night stand October 27, 28, 30 and 31, 2009 — the final show lasting more than three hours thirty-five minutes and including forty-one songs. The *very* last band to perform at the Spectrum, however, was Earth, Wind & Fire when they headlined a private event thrown by Comcast-Spectacor chairman Ed Snider on January 16, 2010.

Harry then offered to take the sticks back, have them signed by Max later that evening and sent to me. For a brief moment I considered it, some vague memory of the Alvin Toffler quote: "It is better to err on the side of daring than the side of caution" running through my mind. But in a moment of clarity, I opted for the latter considering Cervantes' more well-known counsel as the better bet: "A bird in the hand is worth two in the bush."

I thanked him again — for the offer this time — and turned to leave just as he mentioned having to change all the drumheads on the kit.

"I'll set them aside for you if you want them," he added. With no reason to decline, I accepted and he suggested I come back in an hour and he'd have them ready.

I spent the time eating lunch in the seats and watching what few show preparations were still going on. As promised, when I made my way back down behind the stage, Harry had the heads waiting for me and packed in the Remo boxes that the new ones came in. I accepted them graciously and we talked some more as he carefully tuned the new head on Max's snare drum for that night's show. But always mindful not to overstay my welcome, I was soon on my way — though not without a quick walk onstage "just because."

It was both a good start to the new season and a memorable return to the old Spectrum. And though I was happy to have had what I believed at the time to be one last intimate look inside before the doors closed following Bruce's run, in time I'd learn that the announcement of those final shows would prove at least a bit premature as news of the Spectrum's impending demise sparked an interest among artists wanting to play there one last time. Despite this recent set of shows, Bruce was among those who would once again grace the Spectrum's stage before the year was out.

During the first date on his final run more than five months later (October 13, 14, 19 and 20, 2009) I managed to stop by late in the afternoon for one *more* final Spectrum visit. And though it was a relatively positive experience, it ended somewhat unexpectedly.

After making my way down to the stage, again being assembled at the opposite end of the arena as on Day One of those previous dates, I managed to reconnect with Harry, reintroduce myself and find him eagerly offering me another pair of sticks. Within the narrow confines of this particular hobby, I consider them to be of some value as he advised me that they were from the final show at Giants Stadium where, just a week earlier, Bruce and the band closed *it* down with a string of five shows between September 30 and October 9.

I again accepted his offering, tucked them into my back pocket and spent a few minutes in idle drum chat with him before being approached by a guard who took me aside and began questioning me about who I was, why I was there and what I was doing "under the stage near all the guitars and equipment." He asked in such quick succession, however, that I was unable to utter more than a few clipped replies. After this brief but incensed interrogation he walked me through the familiar backstage halls (all the while barking at any security personnel we passed not to let anyone else in without a pass), around to the loading entrance and up the ramp personally seeing to it that I was out the door.

After more than thirty years of Spectrum concerts, often

engaged in innocuous moments evading guards and ushers — all without issue or incident I might add; it's somewhat ironic that my final moments there would have me being escorted out by security.

And although this rather abrupt conclusion to all things Spectrum seemed a bit anticlimactic; no personal mental grand finale, no final walk down Memory Lane, just a quick and brusque escort out the back door — in a rock'n'roll sense it was actually quite fitting... almost welcome.

Almost.

THIRTY-ONE
No Doubt

June 11, 2009

You are remembered for the rules you break
— Douglas MacArthur

Though I was eager for the start of another concert season at the Susquehanna, my initial interest in the first band of the summer didn't reflect that enthusiasm. Although I liked them well enough, admittedly jumping on and off the *Tragic Kingdom* bandwagon when that third album was released in late 1995, I relegated them to airplay-only status thereafter. But with that as the criteria; No Doubt's track record of hits can easily classify any self-proclaimed casual fan as at least slightly more.

As I reflected on what about them appealed to me when considering a visit to the arena, I didn't consider singer Gwen Stefani's good looks or voice (both sometimes reminiscent of 80s Missing Persons singer Dale Bozzio) or even the ten songs it turns out I know quite well. Rather it was the work of drummer Adrian Young. From his clean studio sound and high-pitched tunings to his ska-and-reggae-influenced style (somewhat Stewart Copeland-esque); it was the drums that I found most compelling — perhaps rightly so.

So I decided his stick would be a welcome addition to The Collection and made my first trek of the summer to the Susquehanna.

Though concerned about whether I'd be remembered by those I had come to know in 2008, my arrival was actually met with handshakes and high-fives — and even some friendly hugs and kisses by two of the women. Needless to say I was somewhat taken aback but pleased to know my absence didn't diminish my standing. And as the season rolled on I realized that my perceived status among these connections became practically irrelevant. Clearly a corner had been turned as questions about legitimacy were replaced by casual exchanges and greetings from guards and crew members alike. And though this was certainly a welcome relief a degree of apprehension continued to accompany each visit.

With regard to getting sticks it was a relatively easy, brief and uneventful day as I met opening act Paramore's drum tech on the loading dock soon after reconnecting with the arena staff. After a few minutes of drum talk (and an offer of one of drummer Zac Farro's sticks — an unendorsed, Kelly-Green-inked and splintered *Pro-Mark - Made In USA Hickory - Natural 2B*) he introduced me to Adrian's drum tech... Toast.

Though I never got Toast's real name, we had a pleasant conversation about drums as he showed me Adrian's Orange County Drums & Percussion kit (all white with the exception of a red snare drum — the only OCDP set I'd see all summer) before digging out a nice used stick for me. As with the drums and the entire stage — an intriguingly sleek 60s-style, multi-level, modernist arrangement — the endorsed stick was mostly white with a glossy black butt end and tip (*Zildjian Artist Series - Adrian Young - Select Hickory USA*).

I politely accepted it and, not wanting to hang around until show time, was soon heading home; my new addition in hand and a curiosity about what the remainder of the season held in store.

THIRTY-TWO
Jimmy Buffett: Margarainyville

June 18, 2009

In summer, the song sings itself
— William Carlos Williams

If there's a summer-breeze, tropical-paradise, island-escapism musical equivalent to the gritty, working-class, heartland-rock offerings of Bruce Springsteen, based on genre-specific lyrics, concert duration and longevity it may very well be the work of Mississippi-born Jimmy Buffett. And with an equally sizeable and zealous fan base known as Parrotheads, it's no wonder the reigning king of "Trop Rock" (ironically born on Christmas) often states that he's "managed to keep the same great summer job" for nearly forty years.

Fun Fact: The term "Parrothead" was coined in 1985 by Eagles bassist Timothy B. Schmit, then in Jimmy Buffett's Coral Reefer

Band, when responding to a comment about the devotion of their fans; many of whom wore parrot hats to the shows. Alluding to the equally loyal fans of the Grateful Dead — long known as Deadheads — Timothy referred to Jimmy's fans as Parrotheads and it stuck. He ended his three-year run with the Coral Reefers after Jimmy's 1985 *Last Mango In Paris* tour and reunited with the Eagles in 1994 for their *Hell Freezes Over* tour.

~~~~

As a longtime devotee (dare I say Parrothead) of his music and all that it embodies, I'm also a fan of his longtime studio and touring drummer Roger Guth and, as such, made sure to plan a stop at the Susquehanna that day in the hope of scoring another stick for my collection.

Though I had seen Jimmy in concert a handful of times, this show on the Summerzcool tour would be my first glimpse inside his traveling Margaritaville and I was looking forward to the sights and sounds — both inside and outside the venue. Unfortunately, the feel-good atmosphere that typically accompanies his shows would be dampened quite literally that day as an impending storm threatened from the west. When I arrived the already unseasonably cold, dark and drizzly weather interrupted the usual flow of events and my customary immediate focus on the drums was replaced by a view of giant blue tarps covering practically everything on the stage.

In time, however, they were removed. Not because of an upturn in the weather, but simply because crew members had to tweak knobs, tune drums and otherwise get everything ready for the rain-or-shine event. As the tarps came off, the stage seemed to come alive; plastic coconut palm trees, faux bamboo fences and other actual tropical plants appeared, as did all the instruments — which was particularly appealing to me as Jimmy's music features many forms of percussion. As such, I was able to get a close-up look at (and quickly play) some nice steel drums, congas and even marimba on either side of the drum riser. And when the stage-wide video screen began projecting rolling waves and beach scenes from around the world, the sunny Caribbean feel was complete — and for the moment reduced the contrasting reality to a mere nuisance.

I approached drum tech J.L. Jamison at the kit — a nice seven-piece set of DWs in a deep Red Lava Oyster finish — and asked about a stick. Happy to pull a used one from the stick bag and hand it to me (an eggshell-white, bare-wood-tipped, Jack DeJohnette signature model: *Vic Firth - USA - Jimmy Buffett Tour*), he asked if I played and we spent a few minutes talking drums while he worked on the kit. I soon thanked him and headed toward the backstage loading dock where I passed a golf cart designed to look like a light blue, wide-mouthed "Landshark" (touting Jimmy's brand of beer of the same name); complete with shark fin on top.

Though I considered meeting some friends outside for a bit of tailgating before the show (with a tentative plan to stay for it), the dismal weather — which seemed to quell the spirits of many Parrotheads (not much happening in the way of over-the-top tailgating on this day) — had a similar effect on me and I decided to pass. But weather aside — and whether or not I stay for any of the shows — whenever I leave the arena with a new addition to my collection it's always a good day. *"Fins up!"*

THIRTY-THREE
A Pause for Perspective

Time puts things in proper perspective
— Cameron Crowe

Just as things reached another level toward the *end* of the 2008 concert season, the 2009 summer season seemed to be *starting* well — eventually progressing into other areas (and arenas) and otherwise taking on a more relaxed feel. The "blanket of familiarity" that now existed between the staffers and me seemed cozier than ever and allowed for a slightly more expanded view of the inner workings of these shows.

Of course, my personal interest in the music and focus on stick collecting continued. But I also became drawn to stories from the many drum techs, guitar techs and other traveling crew members I met along the way. Just as an early discovery that the allure of backstage life wasn't quite so alluring (post-show partying excepted as I have no experience there), some firsthand accounts of life on the road from the crews were equally eye-opening. Extended periods away from family and home (rarely do techs get the opportunity to have girlfriends, wives or children with them), the consequent effect on those relationships and the sometimes labor-intensive drudgery of the work itself all contribute to what many roadies consider less-than-stellar conditions.

Though there's a general consensus among these road warriors that traveling and being around what they love most — music — both fall on the plus side of the job, an inherent paradox is a general apathy toward those things when not on tour. Though each has expressed other interests and musical tastes outside the offerings of their employers (though some techs work for agencies and are only on assignment to artists, many others are actually employed by the bands), many find the idea of attending concerts during their down time as less than appealing. By extension — and just as with anyone else — they cite the difficulty of viewing with detachment something with which they're so closely involved. In essence they'd feel as if they were back "at the office."

Just as I can correlate this theory of detachment to my professional life (as most of us likely can with our own), so too am I able to draw a parallel to my music. No matter how many times I've listened to the songs I've written individually or with Upper Level, it's nearly always from the standpoint of when they were written or recorded. A particular lyric I changed during the process, a mistakenly hit microphone while laying down a drum track or even what inspired a given song are some examples of what I tend to focus on rather than just the song itself. Rarely do I listen to my music dispassionately — nor do I believe I can.

In *The Grand Illusion*, Panozzo illustrates this same understanding, albeit from a much more successful point of view: "It's an amazing feeling to hear one of your songs played on the air. Even today, every time I hear a Styx song, it's a rush. My mind always goes back to a rehearsal, or to laying the track, or to some other aspect of recording the song."

Objectivity under these circumstances is at best difficult to attain. But as Davis describes in *Hammer of the Gods,* the late Led Zeppelin drummer John Bonham may have come close when he had his then thirteen-year-old son Jason fill in for him on *Trampled Underfoot* during a 1979 rehearsal at Knebworth. John then went out onto the field to listen to the band play and, somewhat effectively detached at that moment, remarked afterward, "It was the first time I ever *saw* Led Zeppelin."

As the summer continued, so did stories from the road. And by gaining a fresh perspective I reached a new level of appreciation for "a day in the life of a roadie." And though many of them were quick to point out the obvious fun factor in their jobs, they were equally quick to emphasize that they were indeed *jobs* — not just some traveling rock star party with groupies. In fact, many veterans lamented in some detail the bygone days of backstage life in the 80s and early 90s when many of these more established bands were in their heyday… and when both they and the band members were still young and single.

"Now," according to one, "I have just about enough energy to do the work and crash on the bus."

Once again, Jackson Browne attests to the long, hard work of the roadies in *The Load Out*: "They're the first to come and the last to leave…"

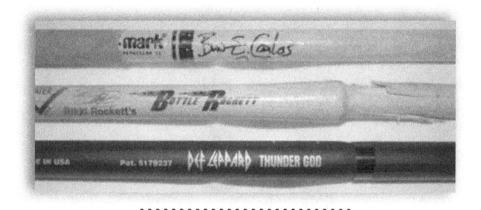

THIRTY-FOUR
Def Leppard / Poison / Cheap Trick: Stage Right II

June 23, 2009

I am a part of all that I have met
— Alfred Tennyson

The summer was starting out well due in part to a decade-jumping representation of artists — Springsteen and Buffett from the flux of the 70s, No Doubt from the booming 90s and now a triple shot from the incomparable and excessive 80s. And as both Cheap Trick (actually a very late-70s band) and Def Leppard became early favorites on either side of my 1978 foray into drumming, it was a show that promised reflection on that time when music was still "newly intoxicating" to me.

Arriving at the Susquehanna in late afternoon on the first day of the tour; coincidentally the same date and arena for Opening Night of the 2006 Journey / Def Leppard tour, I headed inside greeting all the usual suspects and navigating the busy loading dock on my way to the stage. In an odd twist all the gear was already set up and the chaos that usually accompanies this pre-show hour was practically nonexistent. It was, in fact, unusually calm backstage.

Walking to the rear staging area; the section between the onstage gear and the loading dock where empty road cases and miscellaneous equipment linger between bands and where occasional drum sets await their turn in the spotlight, I saw a beautifully-crafted set of Rockett Drum Works (RDW) drums — the custom kit of Poison drummer and RDW namesake president — Rikki Rockett.

In the dimness I stepped in for a closer look and met his drum tech Andy as he handled some last-minute preparations. He invited me to take a seat at the kit for an even closer look and, without question, I found it to be one of the most lavishly, yet artfully finished sets I had seen to date. Random images of skulls and red roses entwined with brushwood all juxtaposed against an aged flaxen background added a sinister element to it. And a shallow bass drum attached to the front of the deeper primary one, oversized wooden hoops and Candy-Apple Red hardware further distinguished it.

Later, as Rikki happened by, I introduced myself and asked about the material structure of the drums. He seemed eager to discuss it saying that the shells are solid hickory and the hoops are a Maple-Walnut mix. He added that RDW also uses other woods and that finishes are unlimited as they custom make everything.

I later called RDW in Los Angeles to get more detail from drum builder Steve Beaver. He noted that the front-end bass drum, which is actually separated from the primary one by approximately two inches, acts as a sub-woofer creating more resonance, ideally in a live setting, without any added impact needed from the pedal. The finish, he added, is actually a single image spread across all the drums. When viewed from certain angles some of the continuity becomes apparent. And as RDW names all the drum sets they make — usually based on the finish — he told me that Rikki named this one *Skullduggery* after the 1983 horror movie of the same name.

When I was done tinkering around on the kit, I asked Andy about a used stick for my collection. He walked me to a road case on the loading dock, dug around and pulled out a nicely-splintered, signature series, wood-tipped *Vater USA Rikki Rockett's Bottle Rockett* custom stick; complete with an unusual and oversized flare-ended grip. As I thanked him he handed me his business card (Drummer, Drum Tech and Drum Teacher) and I wandered out onstage where Cheap Trick was setting up.

Having already met Bun E. Carlos' drum tech Matt on the 2008 Journey / Heart / Cheap Trick tour, I reintroduced myself and reminded him of the stick he gave me. He asked how my collection was coming along and, gesturing toward Bun's latest Ludwig four-piece trap kit in a new Citrus Glass Glitter finish, walked with me to the riser for a closer look.

Fun Fact: All-inclusive drum sets were initially designed as a means of economy, both financial and spatial. And by the early 1900s their playability was improved by the aid of a workable pedal invented by the then-named Ludwig & Ludwig Drum Company. Consisting of a snare drum, a large marching-band bass drum, tom-toms, cymbals and cowbells among other instruments — all mounted to a "contraption" (abbreviated as "trap") around the bass drum — this collective setup came to be known as a "trap kit." Today the term is used primarily in reference to a standard four-piece drum set.

As a Ludwig endorser for more than thirty years, Bun was honored with a Bun E. Carlos Signature Series drum set as part of their 100th Anniversary celebration. The one I was looking at was the first of only fifty made; each personally signed and numbered on the inner-shell label and complete with his personal badge (the emblem on the outside of the shell) and a Ludwig 100th Anniversary badge.

Perhaps the most notable feature of the kit on this day was Bun himself. As he sat on his throne tuning some heads I took the opportunity to introduce myself and shake hands with the man I had first seen in concert more than twenty-eight years prior. We briefly discussed his new drums (with bassist Tom Petersson and singer Robin Zander standing nearby) and I mentioned having seen Cheap

Trick for the first time in 1981.

As the band's chief setlist planner and archivist he remarked with accuracy, "That was the *All Shook Up* tour with Jon Brant on bass."

I also pointed out that it was my first front-row experience and that I had managed it by sneaking down from the third level. Seemingly amused he said, "So you paid for the worst seats but got to see us from the best — that's great."

Though I already had one of his sticks from 2008, Matt offered another and I accepted (my collection can always use more timber). But truth be told, I was just pleased to have met and spent a few minutes with Bun that day; not least because it took place onstage at the drums and right before a show. You really can't beat that with a... well, you know.

In the lull before Cheap Trick took the stage I found myself alone in the rear staging area, unable to locate Rick Allen's drum tech and wondering how I was going to get one of his sticks for my collection. So, with few options and a likely narrow window of opportunity, I decided to seize the moment before it was too late.

All of Def Leppard's equipment was set up and draped in black cloth to conceal it from view. But the drums were mostly visible — and somewhat accessible — from behind. After a quick glance around I slipped inside a small, curtained, vestibule-like area behind the drum riser and saw a stick holder mounted to the drum's rack system. The custom-made Yamaha kit was primarily electronic with an acoustic bass, snare and cymbals (including four sets of hi-hats — one conventional and three centered).

I hopped — seated — onto the drum riser and, leaning forward reached out and grabbed one of the sticks just within reach. I was surprised to see it was another polyurethane one (like Tommy Lee's), but realized this made sense given Rick's condition as a one-armed drummer. Clearly, eliminating any chance of breaking a stick mid-song has to be rather high on his priority list.

The signature model Ahead stick was all black with a white tip and personalized: *Rick Allen - Def Leppard - Thunder God - Made In USA*. An apparent sense of humor is evident by Rick's stick-figure drawing of a one-armed drummer opposite the printed side of the stick.

After the missed opportunity exactly three years prior, I was pleased to finally have this in my collection — however ill-gotten it may have been.

On the way back from placing the day's sticks in my truck I had two chance encounters; the first was with Def Leppard guitarist Vivian Campbell in the backstage lot as he posed for the band's tour photographer, Ash Newell. The second, after watching that photo shoot for a few minutes, was when I made my way back inside to the staging area and I saw Rick Allen standing behind his drum riser wafting incense into the air.

I introduced myself as a fellow drummer and fan since the band debuted with *On Through The Night* in 1980. Easily approachable; he freely answered questions about his drums, the Raven Drum Foundation he founded with his wife Lauren and even why he was burning incense: "It helps create a familiarity and a comfortable, focused place for me when I play."

After he posed with me for a picture he headed backstage as I returned to my seat. And as showtime drew near, the rear staging area began to awaken as other musicians arrived introducing and reintroducing themselves to each other — usually around one or another's instruments.

Poison guitarist C.C. DeVille was hanging out with Rick Nielsen while trying one of his many guitars. Rikki Rockett was pointing out to Bun E. Carlos some of the finer details of *Skullduggery* and Tom Petersson was trying (in vain) to take a picture of his young son, Liam, onstage in front of Bun's kit. Sensing his frustration at trying to corral the little guy, I offered to take a shot of them together and he accepted.

C.C. also cheered on his own young son as he banged around on Rikki's kit while the sons, daughters, wives and girlfriends of other band members walked around taking in all the activity on Day One of this forty-show tour. The entire scene looked more like an extended-family gathering than backstage at a rock concert.

But with three bands of nearly all original members (save bandmates Vivian Campbell and Phil Collen), things weren't so different from a musical perspective. Although everyone was older and families were now a part of the scenery, the performances that night looked very much as they did in years past. The set lists however, nicely complemented by newer material, were a clear indication that this was not strictly a nostalgia tour.

With all these variations and similarities, I'm reminded of a quote by American writer Irene Peter: "Just because everything is different doesn't mean anything has changed."

Cheap Trick opened the show just as some of the guys from Poison and Def Leppard drifted out to watch from the sidelines. It was an interesting show of support as well as an indication that they're still fans apart from being in the business. As we were all in the same area — and as securing this spot onstage was ideal for moments like this — I made sure to make the most of it.

Guitarist Phil Collen seemed genuinely excited to be back on the road and his enthusiastic response to my questions about expectations for the tour were evidence that after twenty-seven years with the band it was all still very appealing to him.

"It's gonna be great," he said. "Three great bands and the whole summer ahead of us — I can't wait to get out there."

If this book has revealed anything, it's that I share and completely understand this continued interest in and excitement about the world of music — both from musician and fan perspectives. Just as I was there to see some of the bands I grew up with, so, too, was he — one of their contemporaries — right there doing the same. Before he left he turned to me and said, "Great talking with you — cheers mate!"

A quick break between songs allowed me to say an equally quick hello to Def Leppard singer Joe Elliott as he stood to my left. Upon mentioning that I had been a fan since their debut album, he replied, "That's really cool — thanks, man," just as the next song began. Soon after, as Joe retreated backstage, C.C. took his spot. And although he didn't stay long, he, too, was getting into the show; applauding and singing along — even posing for a picture with me before disappearing backstage.

A short time later he and the rest of Poison would be out there for a fourteen-song set of hits. And during Rikki's drum solo, C.C. came over to where I was and, in front of a full-length mirror, proceeded to change shirts and spend a few minutes blow drying his hair. It was certainly an unexpected sight; not least because we were only a few yards from the onstage action. After his quick-change routine he strapped on another guitar and headed back out to finish their set.

Def Leppard took the stage to a video retrospective of their career from beginning to present day. From my stage-right vantage point I had an unobstructed view of the stage, the waiting area behind it and a makeshift dressing room beneath the drum riser. It was an interesting perspective as I was able to watch the show as well as some of what occurred between songs or during solos. At one point after bassist Rick Savage changed in the dressing room, he was swapping out his bass and got his hair caught in the guitar strap. It took two assistants a minute or more to untangle him. Later, during Joe's extended song intro on an acoustic guitar — a break in the action usually designed to give the other musicians a rest — Vivian and Rick were laughing together behind the scenes almost as if they weren't in the middle of a show. It was moments like those that grabbed me most; the "real" ones that audiences didn't get to see but which proved the musicians far more human and less the larger-than-life figures they cut in videos and onstage.

There was also an entirely different vibe from being *on* the stage as opposed to in *front* of it. And in some ways this view was like watching a garage band; the de rigueur status of any rock group in its formative years. The wonderful memories from my own such experiences remain fully intact; the sound and feel of that environment unmistakably intimate, unique and raw.

The wide-angle view of the audience offered a chance to see things from the band's perspective and at times I found myself wistfully stealing away into occasional thoughts of "what if…"

In all, this show proved to be one of the best and most interactive for me. As with the previous triple-bill featuring Cheap Trick late last season, I once again experienced a triple hat trick. Only this time it was on a different level as I stayed for the shows and met all the drummers.

Three bands, three sticks and three drummers all in one night; it doesn't get much better than that.

THIRTY-FIVE
August and (almost) Everything After

Scenery is fine, but human nature is finer
— John Keats

July's lineup of concerts passed without much new or of interest to me, so the middle of summer was absent of any visits to the Susquehanna. Then August and everything after came and I found myself right back in the thick of it.

With an even mix of country and rock shows spread out among three venues through September, I kept fairly busy — though not always with designs on going backstage. Occasionally my interest was simply for the shows, other times for the sticks or a soundcheck — sometimes both. Though experiencing *all* aspects of these events is still preferable, it's not always possible as I either arrive too early to justify waiting around or, as is more often the case, I simply have other commitments.

But regardless of reason and no matter the band (as long as I'm interested on at least *some* level); I'm always drawn to the atmosphere and mechanics of a live show. The quiet emptiness of the house, the bustling atmosphere onstage and the maze of road cases, drum risers and miscellaneous gear temporarily crowding the loading dock have all become familiar scenes to me. Crew members zigzag about, summoning assistance or barking orders into shoulder-harnessed, two-way radios while production managers engage various staffers onstage in an ongoing effort to keep the process running smoothly.

Recounting his long-held and like-minded feelings about being in this environment, Guns N' Roses guitarist Slash (*Slash*) said: "Every backstage and soundstage scene that I saw with my mother worked some kind of strange magic on me. I had no idea what was going on, but I was fascinated by the machinations of performance back then and I still am now. A stage full of instruments awaiting a band is exciting to me. The sight of a guitar still turns me on. There is an unstated wonder in both of them: they hold the ability to transcend reality given the right set of players."

By contrast the backstage lot typically seems composed, almost tranquil. And because the fleet of side-by-side equipment trucks is always backed in, the rumblings of activity taking place on the loading dock are muffled to near silence. Gleaming tour buses sit quietly off to the side; only occasionally offering up an artist making his or her way across the lot to the arena. And it's here where I've met a few of these celebrated musicians — always pleased by their responsiveness; intrigued and reassured by their more "civilian" appearance and everyday activities. From a veteran rock singer relaxing with his family outside their bus to a young country star casually tossing a football with a crew member, each lot becomes a surrogate backyard during their time on the road; a place to escape the confines of their temporary home on wheels and idle away the hours until it's time to go to work.

As showtime nears, the local and road crews break for dinner leaving the house nearly empty and the stage strangely hushed. And while the staff quietly awaits the signal that it's "doors open," that distinct calm before the storm once again settles over the entire arena leaving it an atmosphere of peace and tranquility... for the moment.

All of this preparation, which typically begins mid morning and lasts until at least soundcheck (and often again through to show time), is a clear indicator that it's no small feat to pull off a show — much less a full tour — and I've recently come to view the entire display as analogous to an iceberg: the show itself the exposed spire or pyramid — large, impressive and all that most people truly care about despite evidence that it pales in comparison to the much more imposing presence beneath the surface or behind the scenes.

According to NASA's James Overland in *Iceberg*, "Only one-seventh to one-tenth of the iceberg's total mass is above water."

As related to what I have discovered goes into setting up and breaking down a concert, those approximations seem close enough (although I can attest that the exposed "one-seventh" — the musicians' job of playing for a couple of hours — is no easy task either). And though this veiled aspect of the show is not nearly as attractive or exciting as its more obvious counterpart, without it there would *be* no show... just as there would be no iceberg.

Although my collection of drumsticks is dotted with a few I otherwise wouldn't have sought (typically offered by drummers or drum techs from as yet unknown bands), for the most part it represents drummers and bands I admire and grew up listening to or have come to appreciate in recent years. Still, as with any collector who hopes to one day have a complete set (whatever that may be), I still maintain a wish list — though the potential opportunities seem to diminish with each passing year as their respective bands' touring days are infrequent at best.

Then there are those sticks I'm interested in based strictly on the merits of the drummer — apart from whatever appreciation I may have for the band. A drummer's style exclusive of the music can be as appealing to me as a solo work by a guitarist or pianist. When a particular sound catches my ear and compels me to listen even slightly closer, as with No Doubt's Adrian Young, or when I'm referred by a friend to a particular drummer and very much like what I hear, as with DMB's Carter Beauford, that's reason enough for me to value one of their tools of the trade.

It was a mixture of these interests that seemed to make up the next several shows of the season. Whether from Creed or Brad Paisley, Jason Aldean or Journey; each stick was collected for a different reason — and for me each reason was compelling enough to merit inclusion both here and on display.

Creed

August 13, 2009

We are made kind by being kind
— Eric Hoffer

When Creed came to the Susquehanna I stopped in for a quick look around and to see about the possibility of getting a stick as I was fond of drummer Scott Phillips' work on their second album, *Human Clay*. Further, when I read about some of his influences I was pleasantly surprised to discover that Rush and Neil Peart were among them.

I introduced myself to his drum tech, Tony Adams, behind the five-piece set of DW drums (in a Black Ice finish) already set up on the riser. After only a brief exchange he handed me his business card which lists an impressive roster of clients aside from Creed including Matchbox Twenty, Maroon 5 and Puddle of Mudd among several others. And just as quickly we began talking drums.

Shortly into our discussion he brought out a laptop and shared with me some pictures of Creed in the recording studio. Though I didn't expect such an in-depth welcome, it was certainly appreciated and was another reminder of just how kind and agreeable many of these techs have been.

After this warm reception, I was sure The Question would be met with similar treatment and I was correct. Although no used sticks were readily available, Tony handed me a nice, wood-tipped *Vic Firth - USA - CREED - Scott Phillips* signature model and I thanked him accordingly before heading home.

Brad Paisley (& The Drama Kings)

August 15, 2009

Nature provides exceptions to every rule
— Margaret Fuller

Only two days later I was once again back on that stage poking around and looking for collectibles as one of my favorite country artists, Brad Paisley, was in town with opening acts Dierks Bentley and Jimmy Wayne.

For whatever reason, individual country artists (as opposed to bands) seem to use different, albeit very talented, recording and touring musicians on every album or tour. This, and their reliance on songwriting teams to craft much of what they record, leaves a lot to be desired for this purist as my preference has always been what I consider to be true bands; musicians who suffer together through the creative process of writing, recording and touring behind their own material.

Brad is one such musician and, having recorded and toured with his band The Drama Kings since his first album in 1999, he's also one of country's few exceptions to the hired-gun rule. With Tim McGraw (The Dance Hall Doctors) and Jason Aldean (III Kings) as other early and more recent exceptions, he's also in some rather good company.

As I came to know the work of Brad's drummer Ben Sesar over the years, I was hoping to connect with his drum tech, go through the usual process and possibly add one of his sticks to my collection. And whereas a wrinkle in this routine would typically be seen as a negative, that wasn't the case on this day as I made my way to the stage and, in lieu of a drum tech, discovered Ben himself on the riser.

As he was getting situated behind the five-piece set of Cream White Ludwig drums (with a Brass-Tone snare), I approached and introduced myself just as I had with so many drum techs along the way. He was extremely receptive; shaking my hand as I stepped onto the riser and reached between the cymbals. And we launched right into a discussion about drums (as drummers are obviously wont to do), the early days of learning his craft and his time with Brad. After he signed a stick for me (*Vater - Power 5A - Hand Selected Hickory - Russ, Thanks! Take care, Ben Sesar*) — and as Brad had come out by this time — he invited me to stay for the soundcheck.

Standing off to the side by guitarist Gary Hooker, I watched and listened for the next several minutes as they went off on a free-form jam and then ran through the show openers *Start a Band* and *American Saturday Night.* Afterward Gary said, "So, you're a drummer, huh?" I replied that I was and asked why he thought so. "Because Brad is out there (nodding toward center stage) but you were watching what Ben was playing the whole time."

Following the soundcheck I walked over to Brad as he was still tinkering with his Baby Blue Fender Telecaster at center stage. When he took it off I introduced myself and asked for a quick picture with him. He easily agreed — remaining composed even when his tech couldn't seem to work my cell phone camera right away.

After a few tries he got the shot. And as Brad and I shook hands I thanked him while leaning in and offering a muted apology for the delay. He reassured me that it was "no problem… don't worry about it… nice meeting you."

As I turned to leave, Gary stopped me and handed me a few Brad Paisley picks — a bit of icing on the proverbial cake of the day — and I was soon on my way.

Jason Aldean (& III Kings)

August 18, 2009

Perfection is attained by slow degrees; it requires the hand of time
— Voltaire

My nineteen-year-old nephew Jake and I are both Jason Aldean fans. And when it was announced that he'd be opening for Keith Urban on his *Escape Together* world tour, I saw an ideal opportunity to attain Cool Uncle status.

Since meeting Jason's drummer Rich Redmond on the loading dock of the Susquehanna last summer, we remained in touch via occasional emails and texts. Always affable and upbeat (no pun intended), Rich was one of the good guys; not taken with himself and — as one drummer to another — always eager to cheer me on in this writing project. So when the show was announced for Giant Center in Hershey, PA (unfortunately there were no Susquehanna dates), I called him with a request.

I told him of Jake's appreciation for their music, that he recently joined the Navy and that he'd be heading off to boot camp within a few weeks. I then asked if he'd be able to provide backstage passes if I bought tickets and made the two-hour trip. He said he was never sure about passes until closer to show time, but in lieu of that, would be happy to have two tickets waiting for me at the door. It was a generous and much appreciated offer and I accepted. I told Jake of the plan and he was thrilled.

As we approached Hershey on show day, Jake and I were impressed with the simplicity of the area; its easy rural drive, beautiful expanse of farms and wide open sky (save some ominous storm clouds in the distance). And when we arrived in the heart of town, the obvious home to The Hershey Company, the near flawlessness of everything seemed almost surreal and began to amuse us.

After passing a sign touting Hershey as "The Sweetest Place on Earth," we began joking about all this "perfection," albeit with an undercurrent of admiration. From the landscape and architecture of homes, shops and schoolyards to the courtesy extended by other drivers, we were in awe of how downright nice it all seemed.

We began referring to it as Perfect Town, USA and when we noticed that the streetlights all through town were covered with large Hershey Kisses as opposed to standard industrial light covers, we felt our nickname fit, well… perfectly. We kept driving and the laughs (probably of the "you had to be there" sort) kept coming.

When we finally reached Giant Center and paid the parking attendant, she handed me the parking pass and, rather sincerely, said, "Have a sweet day." I thanked her and we laughed once more before heading inside. Clearly, it was time for some music in Perfect Town.

Just prior to the start of the show I saw Rich standing stage side, new sticks in hand and tapping on anything within arms' reach. The seats were great, only one section off stage left, so I walked to the railing to say hello and thank him. Rich shook hands with Jake and engaged him in some discussion about joining the Navy before wishing him well and getting ready to go on.

Afterward Jake was grinning — obviously happy with this stage-side meet-and-greet — and now even more eager to see the show. I was grinning within just to have been able to make it happen.

Before we parted, Rich said, "I'm endorsed now — I have to get you some new sticks for your collection." I replied, "You're *holding* them," and then expressed my usual preference for used ones. "So just meet me here after your set," I said, and he agreed as he headed to the stage.

After a great show that included a cover of Bryan Adams' 1985 number-one hit *Heaven,* we met again at the railing and he handed me the now nicely beat-up *Pro-Mark - Millennium II - Rich Redmond* signature sticks. He thanked us for making the trek, wished Jake good luck again and said to keep in touch before heading backstage with the band.

As Keith Urban isn't on either Jake's or my lists of favorites, we stayed just long enough to see him play the opening song, *Days Go By*, and then left to begin our long ride home out of Perfect Town, USA.

Journey / Rascal Flatts / Dave Matthews Band

September 2009

Charm is a product of the unexpected
— Jose Marti

During the month of September a few of bands from previous summers came through town and I made sure to reconnect with the same drum techs at each.

After Kevin and I saw Journey at the Borgata in Atlantic City (September 4), we met with Deen Castronovo's drum tech Steve Toomey and he accommodated my request for a pair of sticks for Kevin who, in turn, kindly donated one to The Collection. Following a few minutes of drum talk, to include a look at a beautiful Natural Ash wood snare drum he custom made for Deen, I thanked him and let him get back to breaking down the kit as Kevin and I headed home.

When I stopped by the Susquehanna for the Dave Matthews Band later that month (September 20), I reintroduced myself to Carter Beauford's drum tech Henry Luniewski. It was a dismal, cold and rainy Day Two at the Susquehanna for DMB and I helped Henry remove the black tarp from Carter's drum set (the same Jet Black Yamaha kit that he's recorded and toured with for the past ten years according to Henry) while we once again discussed drums, the tour and renovating houses.

When I got to The Question, reminding him of my preference for used sticks, he handed me a new pair from his bag and apologized that no used ones were available. Of course, I was pleased to accept either way and was quick to return Kevin's generosity by donating one of them to his budding collection.

In between those two shows I managed a visit to the Susquehanna for Rascal Flatts on September 11 (with Hootie & The

Blowfish frontman-turned-country-artist Darius Rucker opening). Though Rascal Flatts was not a favorite of mine, I made the effort in part for my neighbor's daughter and die-hard fan, Jamie. Unfortunately, after a failed attempt at getting backstage passes for her from the band's co-manager, Doug Nichols, whom I happened to meet as he was surveying the stage from the seats, her take only amounted to a few guitar picks.

This unsuccessful bid reminded me of the previous summer when Kelley and I took (read: *suffered through*) our fourteen-year-old daughters Alea and Kelsey to a Jonas Brothers show. My effort to bring them backstage with me was unfortunately stopped cold ("No teens allowed back without passes," according to my connection at the gate). So as a consolation prize of sorts I went back myself, made my way to the stage and grabbed a few signature guitar picks for them. Though only small mementos of the night the girls were quite happy with them.

My take at Rascal Flatts, however, was a bit more inclusive as I managed an unexpected meeting with well-respected and longtime drummer and bandleader Jim Riley. Again, though not a fan of the band in a broad sense, I was certainly aware of Jim and had recently read of his recognition as Best Country Drummer and Best Clinician by readers of *DRUM! Magazine* and *Modern Drummer* respectively.

While poking around onstage and asking for his drum tech, Craig, a stagehand pointed him out and I introduced myself. As we discussed the Silver Sparkle eight-piece Ludwig kit, Jim walked out and Craig introduced us. Very outgoing, he volunteered details about his kit, his Ludwig Drums endorsement and what summer on the road has been like. When he suggested I sit behind the kit for a picture with my cell phone, of course I accepted. And after a few more minutes of drum talk, he offered me a pair of used sticks (*Vater 5B - Hand Selected Hickory - Jim Riley - Rascal Flatts*) before we both headed backstage; he to his tour bus likely to rest up for the show and I to my truck to head home.

Although my visit was initially driven by one agenda, another unanticipated one actually came to pass and by all accounts turned out quite well. And though I thought these last few shows marked the end of the 2009 summer concert season, an encore of sorts would soon extend it — and another unanticipated outcome would result.

THIRTY-SIX
A KISS Soundcheck

October 12, 2009

For it is in giving that we receive
— St. Francis of Assisi

With all the sticks, picks, soundchecks and stageside views — as well as a few impromptu meet-and-greets along the way — the 2009 season had proven even more eventful than the previous summer. And just when I thought I was finally going to be able to return to my writing free of any additional excursions, a sign — or marquee as it were — appeared in the distance.

I'm not sure whether it was the potential challenge of a new arena, the possibility of catching a soundcheck or just an opportunity to add another chapter to this book. But the lighted words beckoning to me from outside Philadelphia's Wachovia Center late that day — KISS: Tonight 8:00PM — quickly found me taking the long way home.

It had been more than thirty years since I last saw them at the Spectrum and though they dropped out of favor for me shortly thereafter (once I discovered Aerosmith's 1975 album *Toys In The Attic* as I recall), something about their storied history — and perhaps that early connection to drumming — held sway over me and I was drawn in. But the Wachovia Center was an imposing presence; looming large over the Spectrum and seeming as if it was the concert-hall equivalent to Fort Knox. As such, and with little confidence in my ability to simply saunter in, it had yet to be on my list of targeted sites.

Fun Fact: Although Fort Knox is a well-known United States Army post in north-central Kentucky, the term commonly used in American English to convey incomparable cutting-edge security is actually a reference to the United States Bullion Depository. This fortified vault building stores a large portion of official gold reserves for the United States and is actually located adjacent to Fort Knox.

After an aborted effort to enter via the well-monitored employee entrance (my business attire didn't do the trick this time), I exited and walked several yards to an entrance for one of the Wachovia Center's restaurants. When I approached the door for the sole purpose of getting a glimpse inside, an older, affable guard suddenly opened it saying, "How are you doing, buddy?" Reacting almost instinctively I walked in — replying in kind — and thanked him accordingly. Heading directly to the concourse area then into the house, I quickly made my way down to stage level, stepped on a railing and hopped onstage all in one fell swoop in a matter of a minute or so.

This continuous motion from street to stage was clearly adrenaline induced as it was a new arena for me (for this activity anyway) and, as such, I felt very much out of my element. I found myself in a position of having to keep one eye on my actions and the other on my surroundings — something I haven't had to do in quite a while — while moving in double time in an effort to remain under the radar ("keep moving, get in and out as quickly as possible"). But this compulsory approach actually served me well as, unbeknownst to me at the time, soundcheck was looming.

Once onstage, of course, I headed for the drums — a double bass, eight-piece set of Jet Black Pearls on a drum riser that was, at the moment, lowered to stage level and hidden behind a seven-foot-tall KISS sign. There was just enough room between the sign and the drums to squeeze in and when I did I saw drummer Eric Singer's drum tech, Paul, working. I told him of my Mission and he gladly contributed a pair of signature model sticks right off the left bass drum (used during the Madison Square Garden show two nights prior, according to Paul) — one of them cleanly split at mid-point: *Zildjian - Artist Series - Select Hickory USA - Eric Singer.*

Fun Fact: The cover image of this book, which is a shot of Eric's kit from behind the KISS sign at stage level, was not manipulated in any way. Rather the out-of-focus, mottled look is what I've referred to as a "happy accident." And as soon as I took it I realized I might finally have the cover shot I'd wanted — a vague behind-the-scenes look at what could in essence be any drum set. I then had the publisher replicate the brass in the cymbals for the background color and they stretched a negative of the original image for the background (this same image and process was simply inverted for the back cover).

I thanked him, grabbed a couple of Paul Stanley "KISS Alive 35" guitar picks from Paul's microphone stand (a nod to thirty-five years since the February 18, 1974 release of their debut album) and headed toward the side of the stage on my way to the seats. But before I could escape unnoticed another roadie, clearly annoyed (and rightly so) asked what I was doing up there. Before I could answer he told me to leave with the warning, "You could be kicked out for being up here without a pass!" I offered no explanation or resistance but rather quietly left the stage as I had intended, took a seat and watched as the band eventually came out — uncharacteristically in jeans and t-shirts — for their soundcheck.

With huge "KISS Army" banners hanging behind stage left and right, a wall of mostly-faux amplifiers lining either side of the drum riser (the most literal use of that term on all the stages I've seen as it would actually rise during the show) and a stage-wide video screen, the band members spent a few minutes adjusting their sound before Paul suggested playing "Delilah" — referring to *Modern Day Delilah* off their latest album *Sonic Boom*. As they played, bassist-vocalist Gene Simmons began flicking several picks into the seats.

Though the band disappeared after soundcheck, Gene remained onstage in discussion with his bass tech as I stepped from the first-level seating to the floor for one last look around. As I began to leave, picking up a few of Gene's grey signature picks along the way, I came to the conclusion — rather impulsively — that a look backstage outweighed any need for a hasty retreat (carpe diem!) and, as such, made my way to an access via the barricade at stage left.

Unaware at the time that Gene was simultaneously making his way offstage, I suddenly found myself face-to-face with him in a stageside walkway and, under the circumstances, only mustered a quick and casual, "Gene — nice to meet you." He replied in kind as we shook hands and in his polite, quiet and matter-of-fact manner further stated, "But I'm very sorry, I can't stop right now…" As his words trailed off he continued on backstage, disappearing around the bend and effectively ending our very brief, spur-of-the-moment meet-and-greet.

Rather than leave the way I came in — and as I was already behind the stage anyway — I decided simply to follow Gene's path into the deeper recesses of the arena to see what surprises may await me. Passing a few doorways along the route, four of which were clearly marked "Dressing Room" and each with a respective band member's name beneath, I eventually arrived at the loading dock. Trying not to appear conspicuous or otherwise out of place, I paused and casually looked around — in part to further my adventure but also to get a perfunctory lay of the land in these new surroundings. But seeing nothing of note and having no further reason to be there (other than to possibly cultivate some relationships for future efforts), I decided to quit while I was ahead.

Driving though the parking lot amid a smattering of fans already camped out and tailgating, I stopped and called out to one who appeared to be with his son. Though he approached with a mix of hesitation and curiosity, when I offered one of Gene's picks — suggesting his son might like it — his eyes widened as uncertainty turned to obvious surprise and delight. KISS was his favorite band, as he told it, and he was there that day taking his son to his very first concert. Visibly thrilled to have this little memento to mark the occasion; he thanked me generously, went back to his truck and handed it to his son — whose own delight mirrored his father's.

Though obviously very modest on the surface, there's an inherently qualified value in these souvenirs. Not unlike a foul ball caught by a fan at a baseball game or an autographed program for an admirer at some backstage door, they offer a rare opportunity of connection; occasion to share the spotlight however faint or peripheral. And for my part a sense of satisfaction comes from the slight philanthropic aspect of it; being able to afford that opportunity — my motivation directly tied to thoughts of how I would have felt had someone done something similar for me at a concert thirty years ago. As such, I try to share the spoils whenever possible in the hope that I may make someone's day — and perhaps even "cross-code" a lifelong memory for them in the process.

It was a satisfying late afternoon as two more sticks were added to the mix, another soundcheck was experienced and I quite literally crossed paths with a musician I first discovered during my earliest days of drumming. But equally gratifying, albeit on a different level, was that during this course of events I was able to somewhat dispel my apparently ill-conceived assessment of the Wachovia Center as some daunting, impenetrable fortress — although one incursion does not a sure thing make. And as it turned out, this was something I'd be able to test fewer than two weeks later.

THIRTY-SEVEN
AC/DC: The Final Act

October 21, 2009

> *Still ending, and beginning still*
> *— William Cowper*

Back at the Wachovia Center for what turned out to be the final show of this extended concert season, I was hoping to get in, get a pair of Phil Rudd drumsticks and get out relatively unscathed and hopefully unnoticed — finally free to resume this project unfettered by any further demands on my time. Inviting concerts, enticing marquees and all other appealing, albeit necessary, distractions would be behind me — the relatively open road of writing my only horizon.

    A classic hard rock band and perennial favorite of millions, AC/DC held only a casual interest for me despite their record-setting 1980 release *Back In Black* being both one of the highest selling albums ever and essentially a soundtrack of the times; largely behind the anthemic *You Shook Me All Night Long*. But musically speaking I still count myself fortunate to have seen them once in their original incarnation when they opened for Ted Nugent at the Spectrum in 1979 (only two days after the August 3 release of their previous album *Highway to Hell*). Fewer than six months later lead singer Bon Scott would be dead as a result of "acute alcohol poisoning" and, in what seems to be simple euphemistic rephrasing, "death by misadventure."

I wasn't sensing much of the restless intimidation experienced during my diversion to the Wachovia Center only nine days earlier, though I was feeling bit apprehensive about getting — and being — inside as these were still relatively uncharted waters for me. But that initial exposure during the KISS soundcheck provided a level of relief that seemed to lessen this nervous anticipation and, as such, I forged on.

Strolling around outside the arena wondering how to go about doing whatever it was I was going to do; I paused at an area overlooking the loading ramp where all the tour buses were situated. This less-traveled walkway on the eastern side of the venue was essentially empty, save an employee on a cell phone smoking a cigarette outside a door that was tucked away in a corner. Flicking his cigarette away he ended his call, opened the door and simply entered — no electronic swipe card access, no key and apparently no lock of any type — and I thought to myself, *"Surely, it can't be that easy..."*

After some quick deliberation I decided to follow suit and see where this mystery door might take me. Two descending flights of stairs later only found me confronted by another door. After additional consideration — *do I go in or turn around?* — I breathed deeply and did as I always seem to do; I entered... all the while thinking of that quote: "It's easier to ask forgiveness than to get permission" (US Navy Rear Admiral Grace Murray Hopper). And it was here in this narrow vestibule-like area with a wall to my left, yet another door straight ahead and a large window to my right — behind which were several uniform-clad security personnel — that I was sure to discover my fate.

As I peered through the glass one of the uniforms asked — quite nicely — if he could be of assistance and I replied that I was "looking for the men's room while I wait for one of my trucks to arrive." He explained that the facilities were "just beyond this door and to the left by the vending machines" as he buzzed me in.

"In" was actually an outer concourse area behind the stage where all the inner workings seemed to be happening (almost truly the "engine room" of the show). And when I exited the men's room I found an opening that led directly to the house behind stage left — exactly where I met Gene Simmons more than a week earlier.

Suddenly in the midst of several techs all tending to their respective gear, I openly asked who the drum tech was. Rather than answer me directly, one of them called out toward the stage, "Hey Dickie! You've got a visitor!" Then he pointed to where I could find him up a set of stairs at the drum riser. When I was quick to point out that I didn't have stage access he replied, "No problem," escorting me onstage and introducing me to Dickie.

Phil's drum set, the only Sonor kit I recall seeing since Rich Redmond's (Jason Aldean) back in 2008, was similar to mine with a beautiful Gloss Black finish (though he had Paiste cymbals all around as opposed to my Zildjians). And after a minute or two of drum talk with Dickie, an older tech who has been with the band for many years, I asked about a collectible stick. He was quick to point out that he doesn't give away the aluminum and polyurethane Ahead sticks as "they don't break." Pulling one out to show me (though I was well aware of them from the Tommy Lee and Rick Allen models) he explained how they get refurbished and I quietly listened as he continued in detail. When he finished, I nodded in agreement that it made sense not to give them away.

"I must be asked a hundred times at each show for a stick," he added. "But I can't give them to one person and not all the others." Again, I respectfully said that I understood. Then, unexpectedly, he had a change of heart. "But since you collect them, here — take it, hide it and just walk away. Don't let anyone see it on your way out."

And with that I accepted the all-black *Ahead - Made In USA - Phil Rudd* signature model stick as I thanked him, shook his hand and, heeding his advice, left the stage.

Walking to the front row I paused to take in the immense emptiness of the nearly 22,000-seat arena which only hours later would be so full of life and music. Then, in a sort of curtain call on the season (and on the stories for this book it would seem), I quietly headed out and headed home one final time in 2009. Making sure to thank the guards as I passed, I made my way back through the myriad doors, up the secret stairwell and out to the concourse certain to remember that "mystery door" tucked away in the corner.

Although I passed my own test by managing my way into the Wachovia Center a second time — thus "proving" my first effort wasn't a fluke — I soon recalled an old expression that gave me pause and left me somewhat in doubt; already looking ahead to the 2010 summer concert season likely in an effort to prove something to myself once again: "Third time's a charm."

Although that may very well be, it's unlikely I'll ever consider any potential visit a sure thing. And perhaps on some level that slight uneasiness is precisely why these backstage incursions, explorations and observations have worked out so well… for so long… so far.

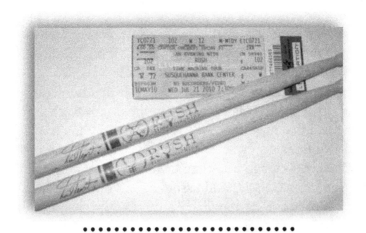

THIRTY-EIGHT
Rush: Une Autre! Un Rappel! Encore!

July 21, 2010

To profit from good advice requires more wisdom than to give it
— Wilson Mizner

Though it was my intention to bring this project to an end following the 2009 concert season and then spend the winter writing, editing and rewriting all the stories, as evident by the date beneath this chapter's telling title I made one exception.

Although I experienced a handful of backstage visits in 2010 and collected a few sticks along the way (Sugarland's Travis Aaron McNabb — *Pro-Mark Millenium II*... Barenaked Ladies' Tyler Stewart — *Regal Tip Groovers*... and for my brother-in-law Chris, Godsmack's Sully Erna — *Vic Firth Rock*), I opted not to write about any of them as I didn't want to delay the completion date of this book any longer.

But prior to the summer when Rush announced dates for their *Time Machine* tour, I knew I had only two choices: either finish writing very quickly and get my manuscript off to the publisher before the tour came to town… or take in another backstage jaunt and at that point feel compelled to put it into words for this book.

Obviously, I don't write quickly enough.

Shortly before arriving on that hot July afternoon, I texted one of my local crew contacts asking if the drums were onstage yet and he replied that they were still being rolled off the trucks. When I arrived, Neil Peart's drum tech Lorne was still in the earliest — perhaps busiest — stage of setting them up (unpacking and placing the acoustic drums, stands and assorted gear on the riser). As such and as in most cases, I remained at a distance and waited for a suitable time to approach.

During my wait I approached guitar tech Scott Appleton and asked about the latest setup he was working on for guitarist Alex Lifeson. Eagerly showing me around his workstation, he went into detail about some of the newest gear (most of which was beyond my comprehension). Then, after I offered him a piece of gum, he thanked me by handing me a few of Alex's varied and custom *Time Machine* signature guitar picks. After thanking him in return, I offhandedly stated that "my friend Kevin is going to appreciate one of these" and he said, "Well then you may as well just give him his own set," as he handed me a few more.

Never of the opinion that I'd made an impression enough to be remembered by any of the drum techs I met more than once, when I finally approached Lorne, I reintroduced myself with reference to the past… the 2004 *R30* tour when he invited me to the riser to take pictures, the 2007 *Snakes & Arrows* tour when we discussed details of the kit and the letter I wrote to him later that year in appreciation for all of the above. It was then that his ears pricked up and he thanked me for that letter saying he'd never before received one from one of Neil's fans. He further noted that it's posted with other tour memorabilia on the wall above his desk in his home office in Vancouver, British Columbia.

The new DW *Time Machine* kit, a Barrel-Stave Redwood (on a matching drum riser) with copper leaf and silver alchemy symbols all around (part of the in-progress Rush project titled *Clockwork Angels*) is as beautiful as it is elaborate. Equally striking are the new cymbals (again, my weakness) and so it was rather gratifying to have been standing alongside Lorne as he unpacked each one, shined it up and placed it on its respective stand.

After a few minutes of drum talk, I thanked Lorne and told him I'd leave him to his work. But before going I followed up with a request for a pair of Neil's sticks for The Collection. His immediate response: "For you? Absolutely." And as he opened a road case drawer exposing several used sticks, he grabbed a pair and handed them to me humorously adding, "... and *these* have his DNA on them!" I replied, "I *do* hope you mean his sweat." He laughed and I thanked him once again for his generosity before heading toward the loading dock to put them in my truck for safekeeping.

The copper-colored markings on the nicely-dented sticks (*Pro-Mark 747 - Hand-Finished USA - Japan Oak - Rush - Time Machine - Neil Peart*) include a different symbol on each (Copper and Amalgamation) and are only two of the seven symbols used in the previously mentioned and as-yet undefined *Clockwork Angels* project.

On my way back in I noticed two BMW motorcycles parked beneath the retractable awning on one of the tour buses... a clear indicator that Neil had arrived. But I simply passed by them and headed back up the loading dock ramp to speak with one of my acquaintances from the local crew. At one point during our conversation I glanced back at the motorcycles and saw Neil casually wiping them down.

Although the equipment trucks adjacent to Neil's bus were idling loudly, I decided to approach and ask him for a recommendation on a private publisher for this book as he had used such services for early works written before his first widely-published book — *The Masked Rider* — was published in 1996.

Upon introduction I extended my hand but he respectfully begged off noting and showing me that his were dirty. I then asked my question about private publishers and he said he wasn't familiar with any. I referenced his use of them on his earliest books and he seemed at a loss for words — what I sensed as somewhat of an unwillingness to assist.

In his defense, however, it was extremely hot and noisy (so much that we had to raise our voices considerably to have this brief discussion) and I was in his private space soliciting advice when his mind was clearly elsewhere — and rightly so.

It was then that I decided to bow out gracefully and somewhat humorously. Patting him on the arm (in lieu of that once-again elusive handshake), I smiled and said, "So I guess what you're saying is, 'Good luck with all of that.' That's cool — thanks anyway and have a great show tonight."

As I turned to leave he said, "If you go to any magazine stand you'll see several publications that cater to that type of publishing. Maybe you'll find something there that'll help you."

I thanked him again as he opened the door and climbed back into his bus. I then made my way out the backstage gate and headed home only to return with Kevin several hours later — by way of the front doors, ticket in hand — for another exceptional Rush show.

As the information-gathering phase of these stories came to a close following this show, I felt a sense of relief as I'd finally be able to more exclusively focus on writing about them. No more interruptions, no more treks to the arenas or emails to send reminding me of details for additional stories — just writing.

The only exception came nearly four months later on November 10 when I passed the Spectrum following a business appointment. As I pulled up to the south side entrance, I noticed an open door (on which was plastered a "Notice of Demolition" by the City of Philadelphia Department of Licenses and Inspections) and decided to take a look inside. Though well aware that the seats were being removed and sold by management, I was still shocked to see the arena in such disarray — unsold seats strewn about, interior glass windows shattered and a large pile of miscellaneous debris on the main floor.

With only the early-evening sun filtering in through windows and doors and as the only person in the entire place, it was a rather moving scene. After a few minutes of soaking it all in, taking a few pictures and grabbing a couple of small parting mementos, I headed home… silently reflective.

Still, closing the proverbial door on anymore stories for this book was easier said than done. And following this Rush show it wasn't long before I began to wonder who the first band of the next

concert season would be... *"and if I did get backstage for it, would I want to include that story too?"*
 Hmm...

Conclusion

Were I to await perfection, my book would never be finished
— Chinese Proverb

A French expression I once read; "Ca en vaut la peine" ("It's worth the trouble"), seems the best summation of how I feel about capturing all these memories and moments in words. Though they don't arrive at some grand destination nor are they likely to resonate with others nearly as much as they do with me, neither of those was the intended result.

Rather my purpose was simply a labor of love; to tell the stories as they were... because *they just are*. Satisfying my fondness for writing, while conveniently sharing experiences surrounding an enduring passion for music, nurtured my spirit and proved to be an ideal undertaking.

From the earliest days of discovery to the most recent few years of "Research & Development" (with reprieves during each off-season), things started out intermittently and became somewhat more consistent as an overall concept came into focus. Regardless how thoroughly enjoyable (though admittedly frivolous) both aspects were, they were diligently pursued and, as such, gradually, methodically — *gratifyingly* — hard won.

With regard to the often slow process of documenting everything, some advice offered by author Stephen King in *On Writing: A Memoir of the Craft* put it in perspective for me —

most likely saying it best and periodically encouraging me when I had neither the energy nor inclination to continue: "Whether it's a vignette of a single page or an epic trilogy like *The Lord of the Rings*, the work is always accomplished one word at a time."

Including many stories but rejecting others I considered short on detail or potential interest proved a demanding assignment that at times left me feeling it may *not* be worth the trouble ("Ca en vaut pas la peine"). If nothing more had come of it than a few summers spent poking around backstage, that may have been tolerable... for awhile. But I knew I'd eventually need an outlet for my thoughts and notes. That said, it's just as well perseverance won out sooner than later. As for my efforts, at first casual then somewhat more tailored, they actually ended up offering more than whatever I may have anticipated had this been a deliberate journey from the start.

Occasional glimpses behind the stage for that always-intriguing view from the other side of the looking glass spawned a few friendships at the arenas... the more than seventy drumsticks acquired along the way (so far) encouraged use of my woodworking skills and I made time to build displays for them... and suggestions to document these experiences prompted thoughts of writing a book to include an examination of my life through the lens of music. Similar to how school assignments were once made more bearable by its infusion, music was now acting as a bridge to other interests and once again proving to be "the inspired focal point."

The eventual ease with which I was able to access and move about the Susquehanna (and the other arenas to some degree) was the result of an established familiarity both with the people and the places — although never taken for granted. Always maintaining a careful sense of time, place and manner in my approach ("never disruptive"), I respected certain boundaries both physical and figurative. But regardless how many times I was able to pull off these little incidents, each was accompanied by a certain measure of anxiety — no matter how slight — which, paradoxically, was less a hindrance and more a help.

Being forced to fly under the radar compelled me to more cautiously and strategically explore... this slowed my approach allowing me to get to know the people I encountered at least slightly better than had we simply exchanged casual nods of acknowledgement… and they, in turn (and however unwittingly), eventually afforded me incrementally easier access ultimately creating the familiarity.

Each visit, though perhaps mundane on paper, was an adventure. From my truck to the stage and back again I never really knew exactly what was going to take place. But being privy to an inside view was usually the upshot no matter how direct or indirect my approach. And the indirect way (read: covert) helped me figure out just how much I could get away with and even when to abandon a particular "operation." Though I never actually had to duck and cover (save once when the local crew guys alerted me to the presence of an ill-tempered security manager and quickly advised me to hide behind a stage-right road case until the coast was clear), my approach was to be as transparent as possible — again, hiding in plain view.

Author James Bennis once said: "Don't just learn the tricks of the trade — learn the trade." As there is no trade to speak of with regard to this particular undertaking, tricks were the only things *to* learn. But meted out in careful measure they served me well and it was my hope that they'd continue to do so with each successive effort.

When it came time to write each of these stories I removed the respective drumsticks from their display in my music room and placed them in front of me on the desk. These simple and prized reminders were physical connections to each moment and I found myself unconsciously fiddling with them as details of the incidents ran through my mind in search of clarity. This whirling and twirling of details and drumsticks became the process throughout and proved helpful both for memory and motivation. The many pictures I took of drum sets, stages and musicians would also aid in this process providing finer points otherwise lost or temporarily buried beneath so many other wide-ranging memories. And occasional reviews of late-night, post-show recap emails (suffered graciously by a few select friends) further assisted my ongoing pursuit of accuracy.

This all-embracing affair with music — as fan, drummer, songwriter, "explorer" and writer — has been both enduring and inspiring. And as with the other constant in my life — words — music (and all its peripheral connections) has enriched me; providing an outlet for my creativity, stamping my memory countless times and otherwise offering a sense of fulfillment through varied measures of delight, melancholy, amazement, escape and instruction for the better part of thirty years.

Having finally arrived at the end of this project feels like a feat of equal parts preparation, determination and exhaustion (though I may be selling that last one a bit short). Whereas I find the notion and the active process of writing quite enjoyable, in an ironic twist soon after beginning I feel eager to complete whatever piece I'm working on (especially true for this book — as previously noted the first undertaking of its size and scope for me). Contrary to *reading* an enjoyable book where I wish beyond possibility that it won't end, *writing* one is altogether different as I find myself hoping — seemingly beyond comprehension — that it will.

On the other hand, I subscribe to the Chinese proverb that "the journey is the reward" and, as such, take great satisfaction in having turned sizeable concepts into digestible stories and muddled thoughts into coherent words — in essence having narrated these events as clearly, effectively and engagingly as my abilities allowed. And though the outcome may be far from perfect (or even engaging for that matter), I'm pleased to have finally accomplished my goal.

And that, too, is a very acceptable — and respectable — reward.

Acknowledgements

Though we set out alone on many journeys in life, we can often point to family and friends who cheer us on in word and deed as we move toward a goal — be it personal, professional or otherwise. And when the venture isn't a full-time gig it can take exponentially longer to accomplish; seizing a great deal of free time, diminishing the enthusiasm of those "cheerleaders" and even straining family ties.

But I was fortunate to have had unwavering support throughout the more than three years I spent on this book. Although there were a few bumps in the proverbial road when my self-imposed writing exile (and all unforeseen delays) tested the patience of family and the confidence of friends, it was ultimately their continued interest and support that saw me through. As such, and in no particular order, I'd like to express here my appreciation to each of them.

From an unexpected introduction in 1977 to the subsequent discovery of a common interest in music, Dan Hopper and I began our musical journeys together while forging a lifelong friendship. When he picked up a guitar, I picked up drumsticks and during the next several years we learned our respective crafts. Though time and miles eventually found us on divergent paths, our friendship remained intact and through the years we even managed to occasionally reconnect musically.

Unfortunately, Dan was diagnosed with Amyotrophic Lateral Sclerosis (ALS / Lou Gehrig's Disease) in early 2009 and has since lost much of his manual dexterity — including the ability to play guitar. We last played together in 2007 during an offhand reunion of Upper Level (with original members Kevin Bothwell and Chris Rapkin); some of which was digitally tracked and recorded. Hopefully those sessions will be revisited and mixed sooner than later as testament to our last collaborative effort, however brief and unfinished they may have been.

Although our joint playing days are past us now, Dan and I will always share the distinction of having discovered our passion together. And for his part in my history (musical and otherwise), its inclusion in these pages and his interest in seeing this book completed, I thank him.

As with all things music related that I've ever been in involved with, Scot Ward has been the ultimate supporter, advisor and motivator. Undoubtedly one of the most passionate music fans I know, he's always been excited about hearing any new material from me (sporadic though those occasions have been) and enthusiastically engages in detailed discussions about rock'n'roll from all genres and decades. More recently he's been a champion of this book; as eager to read it (and offer advice along the way) as I've been to write it.

Though we've lived on opposite coasts for nearly thirty years (save when I lived with him in 1984 while testing California's musical waters), his loyalty and dedication to our more than thirty-year friendship is rivaled only by the ever-apparent love and devotion he has for his family. As he would say: "Oh yea, no doubt!" For his steadfast friendship, continued interest in these stories and infinite patience while I captured them all in words, I thank him.

As my previously-noted "pseudo partner in crime" — in *front* of the stage at concerts, *on* the stage in bands or *behind* the stage exploring — Kevin Bothwell has been almost as much a part of my musical history as I have. Whether playing together for the first time in an early-teens garage band experiment, reconnecting at a concert nearly ten years later or being the main collaborator on most of the music we recorded in Upper Level and beyond, he's been there nearly every step of the way.

When Kevin first suggested I document all these backstage experiences, he inadvertently positioned himself as one of the "lucky" few who would later have to suffer my detailed email recaps following each show. Despite that, he remains one of my most trusted friends and musical partners (one of the people I noted earlier who have maintained an active interest in music). He's also a contributor of two sticks to The Collection (Dean Castronovo / Journey at the Trump Taj Mahal and Sonny Emory / Bruce Hornsby at the House of Blues — both in Atlantic City, NJ), a formidable competitor in our occasional sport of texting song-lyric trivia and the spark of inspiration behind this book. For all of these things, I thank him.

Writing anything of length, particularly a book, is an intense practice not to be done in short bursts or so sporadically that the groove is lost — or worse — never found. It demands prolonged attention at regular intervals in order to come to its finest realization. The parallel to professional and family life is apparent here and, as such, is a recognized challenge to the leisure-pursuit writer (or musician or artist or actor...). Though finding a healthy balance between creative and practical endeavors is the ideal; it's not always so easily achieved.

Although much of my discretionary time during the past few years has been consumed by this project — taking me away physically (to my home office) and mentally (lost in thought about expression and phrasing) — I'm fortunate to have had my beautiful wife Kelley and our equally beautiful twin daughters Alea and Kelsey at my side throughout. When I assumed the role of writer and disappeared accordingly, it was Kelley who held down the fort and, for better or worse, allowed me time to do my thing. Simply stated, without her this book would not have been completed.

And though my concentrated approach tested their collective patience (and truth be told mine as well), Kelley and the girls ultimately allowed me to come through it relatively unscathed. For all of this — as well as for their continued love and support — I thank them.

Worthy of "Honorable Mention" in this section are a few friends who, along with others who have contributed to my history, are no less appreciated for their efforts and input along the way — as friends, fellow music fans and ardent supporters of this project; my own little "exercise in self indulgence."

Paul Paetow... who accompanied Dan and me to our first Spectrum concert in 1978 (Boston) and, nearly seventeen years later, made possible my first opportunity to see a soundcheck (Van Halen) in that same arena. Paul is one of my closest lifelong friends and we fondly maintain a like-minded — albeit clichéd — view of those formative years simply enough as "the good old days."

Tom Wardach... a friend since middle school with whom I've reconnected on a more regular basis in recent years. As an avid music fan with an equally keen interest in behind-the-scenes accounts, Tom has been intrigued by these stories as they've unfolded on the pages and has even generously contributed a stick to The Collection (Jeff Neal / Boston at the Verizon Wireless Amphitheater in Alpharetta, GA).

Jim Sandercock... my former co-worker-turned-friend and one of the more well-rounded music fans I know (and the person who connected me with his good friend, musician-singer-songwriter Scot Sax). Jim casually took up the cause of pushing for a finished manuscript from me, periodically checking on my progress and even setting a deadline for me (which, of course, I missed). I hope soon to be of like encouragement when he publishes his book on quips, quotes and assorted wordplay.

Final Fun Facts

Although I've attended nearly one-hundred-fifty concerts in big arenas, small clubs and everything in between since 1978, not all of them are covered in these pages. But of those that are included (donated sticks as well), they're represented here by 75,564 words, 273 pages, 103 bands, 75 drumsticks, 47 drummers, 44 guitar picks, 26 guitarists and 43 shows at 12 arenas in 4 states (23 at the Tweeter Center/Susquehanna Bank Center in Camden, NJ... 7 at the Spectrum in Philadelphia, PA... 3 at the Wachovia Center in Philadelphia, PA... 2 at JFK Stadium in Philadelphia, PA and 1 each at the Cal Expo Amphitheater in Sacramento, CA... the Giant Center in Hershey, PA... the Borgata in Atlantic City, NJ... Caesars in Atlantic City, NJ... House of Blues in Atlantic City, NJ... the Verizon Wireless Amphitheater in Alpharetta, GA... the Trocadero in Philadelphia, PA and the 23 East Cabaret in Ardmore, PA).

Along the way I've seen some interesting things on all sides of the stage. And as words and phrases are an obvious draw for me, I took special note of the many humorous messages printed on t-shirts worn by various roadies throughout the seasons. Following are ten of my favorites in no particular order:

No sticks, no picks, no set lists — beat it!
Another free black t-shirt for the roadies.
Which way to catering?
Don't talk to me — I'm working.
Yes I *do* know what all those knobs do!

Bad stagehand — no donut!
It's OK — I'm with the band.
No I *don't* have a guitar pick!
Groupies wanted — no experience necessary.
Blame it on the local crew.

And finally, in the spirit of all of this drum talk and drumstick collecting — and because I mentioned that there are still some sticks I'd like to have in my collection but have yet to acquire — I offer below my "wish list." In no firm order of preference (I quickly found that to be a difficult task to accomplish), it lists only those drummers I admire individually or through the music they're primarily associated with and who are still with us as of this writing. I hope to be able to check off some of them in the coming years… you know, before all of this begins to get out of hand and a bit juvenile…

Alex Van Halen (Van Halen)
Stewart Copeland (The Police)
Ringo Starr (The Beatles)
Liberty DeVito (Billy Joel)
Larry Mullen, Jr. (U2)
Joey Kramer (Aerosmith)
Steve Smith (Journey)
Kenny Aronoff (John Mellencamp)
Phil Collins (Genesis)
Myron Grombacher (Pat Benatar)
Bill Bruford (Yes)
Stan Lynch (Tom Petty & The Heartbreakers)
Roger Taylor (Queen)
Keith Carlock (Steely Dan)
Charlie Watts (Rolling Stones)
Chester Thompson (Genesis - touring)

Art is never finished, only abandoned
  — *Leonardo DaVinci*

References

Adler, Steven and Spagnola, Lawrence J. *My Appetite for Destruction: Sex & Drugs & Guns N' Roses.* New York, NY: HarperCollins, 2010.

Benatar, Pat and Bale-Cox, Patsi. *Between a Heart and a Rock Place.* New York, NY: HarperCollins, 2010.

Bruford, Bill. *Bill Bruford: The Autobiography.* London, UK: Jawbone Press, 2009.

Copeland, Stewart. *Strange Things Happen: A Life with The Police, Polo and Pygmies.* New York, NY: HarperCollins, 2009.

Davis, Stephen. *Hammer of the Gods: The Led Zeppelin Saga.* New York, NY: Berkley Boulevard, 1997.

Fox, Michael J. *Lucky Man: A Memoir.* New York, NY: Hyperion, 2002.

Iacoboni, Marco. *Mirroring People: The New Science of How We Connect with Others.* New York, NY: Farrar, Straus and Giroux, 2008.

King, Stephen. *On Writing: A Memoir of the Craft.* New York, NY: Pocket, 2000.

Kinser, Wiltold. *Hokusai's Great Wave*. Kinser's Personal Site, http://www.ee.umanitoba.ca/~kinsner/about/gwave.html, 1996-2007.

Lamott, Anne. *Bird by Bird: Some Instructions on Writing and Life*. New York, NY: Anchor, 1994.

Levitin, Daniel. *This Is Your Brain on Music: The Science of a Human Obsession*. London, UK: Plume, 2007.

Nuland, Sherwin B. *The Art of Aging: A Doctor's Prescription for Well-Being*. New York, NY: Random House, 2007.

Overland, James E. *Iceberg*. World Book Online Reference Center: World Book, Inc., http://www.worldbookonline.com/wb/Article271040, 2005.

Panozzo, Chuck, and Skettion, Michele. *The Grand Illusion: Love, Lies and My Life with Styx*. New York, NY: AMACOM, 2007.

Pausch, Randy and Zaslow, Jeffrey. *The Last Lecture*. New York, NY: Hyperion, 2008.

Peart, Neil. *Roadshow: Landscape with Drums — A Concert Tour By Motorcycle*. Cambridge, MA: Rounder, 2006.

Peart, Neil. *Traveling Music: The Soundtrack to My Life and Times*. Chicago, IL: ECW Press, 2004.

Phillips, Mackenzie. *High on Arrival*. New York, NY: Simon Spotlight Entertainment, 2009.

Slash and Bozza, Anthony. *Slash*. New York, NY: HarperCollins, 2007.

The Blank Page by Russ DiBella, © 1989 Reaction Time Magazine. All rights reserved.

Just One Moment words and music by Russ DiBella and Kevin Bothwell, © 1992. All rights reserved.

Let It Be words and music by Paul McCartney and John Lennon, © 1969. All rights reserved.

A Matter of Time words and music by Russ DiBella and Dan Hopper, © 2005. All Rights Reserved.

Untamed Hearts words and music by Russ DiBella and Aldo Donato, © 1994. All Rights Reserved.

Does She Know words and music by Russ DiBella and Kevin Bothwell, © 1986. All Rights Reserved.

About The Author

Russ DiBella is a leisure-pursuit writer and musician with a Bachelor of Arts degree in Communications / Journalism from Glassboro State College (now Rowan University).

As an avid reader and writer he has written everything from inspired works of poetry, prose and song lyrics to the more unyielding requirements of professional documents and freelance feature articles for local newspapers during the past twenty-five years. This is his first book and is the culmination of all his writing experiences to date.

Professionally, DiBella has been in outside sales for nearly twenty years and resides in Southern New Jersey with his wife and twin daughters.

CPSIA information can be obtained
at www.ICGtesting.com
Printed in the USA
BVHW031926261120
594297BV00008B/51